Hidden Challenges

Hidden Challenges

Human Dynamics in Organizational Change and Recovery

Editor

Elizabeth Florent Treacy

Contributors

Theo van Iperen, James Hennessy, Fernanda Pomin, Ross Emerson, and Ricardo Senerman

BUSINESS EXPERT PRESS

Leader in applied, concise business books

Hidden Challenges:
Human Dynamics in Organizational Change and Recovery

First published in 2022 by
Business Expert Press, LLC
222 East 46th Street, New York, NY 10017
www.businessexpertpress.com

ISBN-13: 978-1-63742-307-3 (paperback)
ISBN-13: 978-1-63742-308-0 (e-book)

Business Expert Press Service Systems and Innovations in Business and Society Collection

First edition: 2022

10 9 8 7 6 5 4 3 2 1

In memory of Frederic
  —Elizabeth Florent Treacy

In memory of Cor and Nell
  —Theo van Iperen

To Marc
  —James Hennessy

To Claudio, Henrique, and Juliana
  —Fernanda Pomin

To Margaret and Erika
  —Ross Emerson

To Ximena, Ilan, Yael, Eitan, and Dan
  —Ricardo Senerman

Description

When conditions are stable in organizations, the saying goes: "statistics are enough." However, a purely rational-structural way of looking at organizations has never been a sufficient framework for understanding change in organizations. When everything goes crazy, we need all the data—including what might be less visible. People in organizations often refer to metaphors such as "elephants in the room" or "taboos" or "unspoken truths." How can we access the less visible data that these metaphors hint at, and how do we work with it?

The unifying "red thread" of this book is the study of the multiple realities and intersecting social systems that make up organizations. In this book, we do not try to fix organizational challenges. Instead, we seek to shed light on circumstances which otherwise might appear undecipherable or even insurmountable.

Although as a reader, you may choose to dip in and out of the book; collectively, the chapters illustrate hidden dynamics that create energy or inertia in organizations in times of crisis and change. Each chapter author offers concluding thoughts that he or she has found useful in context, not as a solution, but as a pathway for further exploration and experimentation.

Our purpose with this book is to show that leaders and followers in organizations can uncover and frame the dynamics that influence crisis and change at individual, group, and organizational levels, in ways that are pragmatic and applicable. The chapter authors bring us much richer and deeper insights into the "why" behind thorny organizational dilemmas. They show us that if we explore the "why," we may advance toward "how": pragmatic and sustainable options for change.

A key contribution of this book is to show that businesspeople can indeed conduct research into the less visible aspects of organizational life and also put this approach into practice in organizations. All of the chapter authors are not only senior executives or organizational consultants but also graduates (with Distinction) of INSEAD's Executive Master in Change (EMC) program. The chapters are drawn from their original MA thesis research. The contributors offer real gifts: insights and renewed energy to change the way we live in the world of work.

Keywords

systems-psychodynamic study of organizations; cumulative crisis management; organizational nostalgia and postalgia; working with narcissistic leaders; vilification of leaders; leader self-reflection; agency in organizational change and recovery

Contents

Foreword

Erik van de Loo and Roger Lehman[1]

The many significant questions, challenges, and problems that face humanity cannot be solved by increasing our efforts to become even more rational, logical, and systematic. Logic and rationality are required, but in many cases not sufficient to understand both the very nature of a situation and effective ways of addressing it. Complexity—particularly in times of crisis—demands a collaborative and integrated approach.

We argue that for problem analysis and solutions, it is necessary to learn to integrate causal and associative thinking. Whenever we approach a question by asking "why," we activate causal thinking. This implies that we will be able to identify causes—or even better, *root* causes—which in turn provide us with certainty and definitive solutions. Although this process may seem effective in the short term, any situation or challenge in which human beings are involved almost always requires us to incorporate a fundamentally different and additional approach: associative thinking.

The majority of individual and collective behavior and decision-making processes operate from an associative base, which is often not acknowledged, or may be completely disregarded. In our individual and collective behavior, we link (nonlogical) feelings, thoughts, memories, images, experiences, insights, impulses, and phantasies in an associative way.[2] They apparently just seem to come, consciously as well as unconsciously, to mind. This happens in all of us, whether we are aware of it or not, and it reflects an aspect of the beauty and organic emerging nature of the human experience. In our opinion and experience, awareness of the associative nature of these elements is a distinctive quality of successful problem solving.[3]

The capacity to integrate causal and associative thinking, as a source for addressing personal, organizational, and societal questions, needs to be developed. Leaders, professionals, consultants, and coaches need to learn to use themselves as an instrument, by integrating causal and associative thinking in the first place in themselves, as a precondition for enabling this in groups or teams. This predictably also often activates strong resistance—in individuals and in groups—against making these links between rational and associative and between conscious and unconscious. Paradoxically, in solving problems, we both have a wish to discover the new and at times a need to not know and avoid discovering. And to complicate matters, this is not a conscious decision but an unconscious defense mechanism.

Since 2000, the INSEAD Executive Masters in Change, previously named Coaching and Consulting for Change, is a program designed to equip professionals and leaders with the knowledge, concepts, and methodologies necessary to integrate and apply this more holistic approach—integrating the logical and causal with the associative elements that coexist less visibly—with real team, organizational, and societal issues. We are very appreciative that five graduates from this program have each contributed to this book meaningfully with their individual application and analysis of real-world organizational challenges. Their five cases are very helpfully preceded by an introductory chapter by Elizabeth Florent Treacy on the fundamental premises and characteristics of what has come to be known as a "systems-psychodynamic" approach to exploring life in organizations.

This book reflects the importance of a joint effort. The seriousness and complexity of all the issues at hand demand a collaborative and integrated approach. We trust that this book will be a source of inspiration and insight for leaders and professionals who are committed in their search for helping teams and organizations to adopt a more integrated approach to change.

Acknowledgments

The foundation of this book was laid at INSEAD's Fontainebleau campus, where together we spent so many treasured hours during our Executive Master in Change (EMC) program. On our collective journey from June 2017 until December 2018, we discovered new frontiers and opportunities in ourselves and in our interactions with the world.

Our first and deepest gratitude goes to the people who made this great adventure possible: our colleagues from Wave 25; Program directors Professor Roger Lehman and Professor Erik van de Loo for their guidance and for the Foreword they contributed to this book; and the faculty and staff who challenged and supported us. We also want to thank each other, the coauthors of this book. Despite the differences in our professional backgrounds and personalities, we managed to write a book we can feel proud of.

In addition, Elizabeth wants to recognize the seminal contribution of Manfred Kets de Vries, Gilles Amado, and Anton Obholzer, not only to the field of systems-psychodynamics but also to her own professional and personal development. As the lead Editor of this book, she acknowledges the professional, dedicated, and empathetic work ethic of the group of chapter authors who brought this book to life. On behalf of the chapter authors, she thanks Scott Isenberg and Jim Spohrer at Business Expert Press for their warm and encouraging support and feedback, as well as their professional approach to working with practitioner–researchers such as ourselves.

Theo wants to thank the people of ABN AMRO Bank who were kind enough to receive him and allow him to test his concepts of organizational recovery. A distinct word of thanks goes to Gerrit Zalm—ABN AMRO's former CEO—who showed courage and generosity by appreciating Theo's suggestion to use their recovery case for his study.

James wants to acknowledge all those he has worked with, past and present, who contributed their dreams and longings for his study of an organization in transition. Their hopes, fears, and above all, love for their organization shone through.

Fernanda thanks and acknowledges each one of her research participants who shared with her their personal—and often painful—experiences dealing with a narcissistic leader. She is grateful for the opportunity to learn from their experiences and hopes that their courage to share their stories may help others who are also struggling to navigate narcissistic leadership.

Ross thanks all his research participants who shared their very sensitive and personal stories with him. Without their trust, courage, bravery, honesty, and vulnerability, his research and the new insights gained would not have been possible.

Ricardo thanks all those who helped him realize the dangers of working at speed without making time to reflect properly. He is grateful for all his guides who encouraged him to search for ways to live a busy life of an executive while also managing stress effectively and developing the ability to see things from different perspectives.

Together, the authors hope that this book will be of use to both individuals and organizations that are going through their own hidden challenges dealing with crisis and change.

CHAPTER 1

Deciphering the Human Mysteries of Organizational Life

Elizabeth Florent Treacy

Crisis and Change in the Organizational Context

We are all learning to live within a continual state of global upheaval. We contemplate previously unimaginable near-future possibilities that range from climate catastrophe to civilian space travel. We face challenges of crisis and change that have never been paralleled in all of human history.

Not so long ago, the scope of working life for most people was limited primarily to fields, flocks, or factories. With the tragic exception of war, there was comparatively little interaction between countries on a global scale. The Great Man theory of leadership prevailed: if you could get a capable man—an authoritarian leader—at the head of a village or a company, the rest would fall into place.

Today, the world is in a complex, and most likely permanent, state of "stable instability or instable stability."[1] Many people in organizations would say this is good news. Change, in that context, is often seen as being exactly what is needed. "A new broom sweeps clean!" or "It is easier to change people [fire and hire], than to change people [their way of working]."

But the organizational challenges we face now are radical, hard to foresee, and difficult to mitigate—as any organizational leader will admit if you ask what gives him or her nightmares. Those challenges can be deeply intimidating and disturbing for leaders and followers; indeed, psychological distress and related reactions are augmented when a person or group is under stress.[2] It is no longer possible for anyone at the head of a business to remain a detached observer, objectively making decisions. Their most frequent question is: "How can I—a key player in my organization—possibly manage this? What am I supposed to *do*?"

In particular, in situations of crisis and change, *people* behave in unpredictable ways. One senior executive recalled that he was shocked by pandemic-related interactions with his colleagues. Shaking his head in disbelief, he said, "I saw chaos. I saw how mature, educated people can create chaos." In fact, what he saw was people seeking to divert the focus of attention to irrelevant or alternative issues, in order to distract themselves from the pressure and intensity of the situation.[3] Indeed, paradoxically, the common tendency toward survival behavior when under pressure adds yet another source of complexity in periods of disruption.

In the final analysis, crisis and change are increasingly difficult because for organizations in the 21st century, everything and everyone is interrelated, and every interaction creates unpredictable consequences. No single individual can control the functioning of the whole, but one single individual can be the source of a great deal of trouble on a very large scale.

The fundamental challenges of crisis and change in organizations today can be understood and effectively managed by tapping into the broader, more holistic view that a "systems-psychodynamic" approach provides. This view includes three "fields": the environmental context and organizational system, groups of people in organizations, and what is going on inside each individual.

This holistic perspective allows us to explore the interrelatedness of these three elements. The term *systems* refers to context and environment: the forces from "outside" as well as the system "reality" that is created by the dynamics of small and large groups.[4] *Psychodynamic* refers to the underlying, out-of-awareness motivational factors and past experiences that influence individuals' beliefs and behavior patterns. This approach considers what is "within": the inner world of individuals, including their emotions. ("Psychodynamic" is the term preferred by organizational practitioners, as it reveals how the forces of the unconscious are dynamic, not passive. This term also moves away from the treatment and pathology orientation of psychoanalysis.[5]) This holistic approach gives us a lens

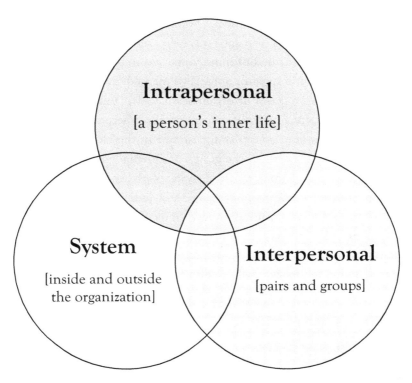

Figure 1.1 The overlapping spheres of dynamics in organizations

for including both the "visible and measurable" and the "unspoken or unseen" in organizations (Figure 1.1).

Viewed this way, one sees that an organization is not a machine; it is a collective conversation[6] created from shifting, ambiguous relationships between people and their environments. Patterns of action—decisions, indecisions, paranoia, and delusions—emerge from human relationships. When people or organizations are stressed by change or challenged by crisis, these patterns of action—if left hidden and unmentioned—will generate tension and anxiety. Therefore, in the face of crisis and change, a leader cannot direct events in isolation. An employee or stakeholder cannot remain passive and hope for the best, or alternatively, create a cloud of chaos as a distraction technique. Everyone has to be aware of their own power and influence within the system and take responsibility for their own participation.

The systems-psychodynamic approach brings three valuable aspects to the topic of managing adversity and change. First, it is a rigorous and valid method of inquiry and research—a way to *analyze* what is happening in organizations. This method gives us a view into the unconscious processes of organizational life, "one of the dimensions most resistant to scientific investigation."[7] Second, it enables us to *decipher* what goes on under the surface in the reciprocal zone of influence where the system, the group, and the individual are susceptible to tension and anxiety.[8] Third, systems-psychodynamic methods inform *practical applications,* ranging from individual reflection and review to group or organization-level interventions such as culture change or crisis recovery. In short, an emphasis on unconscious and emotional processes equips us to "address organizational change and the psychological forces which it unleashes."[9]

A Sliver of Light

When asked about his experience with the systems-psychodynamic perspective, one CEO, we'll call Jack, offered the following story. He recalled the period when he landed his first CEO role. Coming on board, one of his challenges was to carry forward the unifying aspects of the founder's legacy, while making the organization relevant in the future. After several years of running a "best place to work" survey, Jack noticed with frustration that the results had been the same year after year. No surprises—and no change. The consultants who officiated over the survey ran the numbers and determined that there were four key drivers that the company should focus on in the coming year, in order to improve things. Next year, same results—despite well-intentioned activities and efforts aligned with the identified drivers, no change.

Jack had an epiphany. Instead of looking out of the metaphorical window, hoping to see prophets on donkeys arriving in the form of external consultants, he and his team would, instead, go down to the factory floor and explore what was going on, or more to the point, what was *not* going on. It soon became obvious that the employees had little emotional connection with the survey questions; they couldn't see an outcome linked to the input; and the whole organization had become, paradoxically, addicted to, and dismissive of, the yearly results.

Jack and his team decided to demote the one-size-fits-all consultant emphasis on the four key drivers (which nobody really understood anyway), and instead, focus on a bottom-up approach. They empowered employee work teams to describe and explore the challenges that *they* believed were key in order to have a best place to work. The employees knew very well that they didn't need a lovely-dovey feel-good exercise, but to focus on a place where the real work of facing the future could be accomplished. Within a year, they had drained the swamp and gained a clearer view of the landscape. The employees felt listened to and safe to innovate, which they did in many key areas very quickly. "Surveys are the crack cocaine of marketing and leadership," Jack concluded. "We love quantitative data! It's deterministic and certain! The light is red, or it's green!" It does just enough to alleviate the pain in the system by distracting people and convincing them that they are taking action. However, the problem with statistics, he said, is that people are overwhelmed by all the data. It's not alive, or it is only active in specific silos. It does not speak to people's hearts. How do you join it all up? How do you know what you don't know? What is missing?

Jack had come to understand that as CEO, he needed *all* the data, including what is not captured in a survey: the employees' hopes, fears, and fantasies. He joked that it is like looking for the bathroom in the middle of the night. If you can see a sliver of light escaping under the door, then you know you are heading in the right direction. If you can find that door, then you are in the light and you can get down to business. Staying tuned to less-visible dynamics in the organization, he concluded, is like being able to see the light under the door.

Jack is in good company. An increasing number of businesspeople have come to realize that the use of systems-psychodynamic concepts can provide greater insight into organizational challenges at all levels. This perspective renders less-visible realities more accessible and worthy of interest.[10] In addition, it offers novel and often startlingly original insights.[11] In sum, systems-psychodynamics "represents arguably the most advanced and compelling conception of human subjectivity that any theoretical approach has to offer."[12]

As Jack discovered, this approach is particularly adapted to making sense of periods of disruption during which emotions resonate, echo, or are baffled and dampened, within individuals and among the various levels of an organizational system.

The Five Premises of the Systems-Psychodynamic Approach

The systems-psychodynamic worldview encompasses dynamics that can be imagined as moving from the outside-in (the *system*, including elements such as the organization, the industry environment, and the economic climate), within groups (the *interpersonal*, from two-person dyads to large groups), and from the inside-out (the *intrapersonal*: individual, internal). It illuminates and informs studies and interventions in real-world contexts and organizations; it is not limited to theory. It describes and facilitates emotional forces and transition, and therefore it is particularly relevant in the context of crisis and change. It informs us: *There is a rationale behind every human act—a logical explanation—even for actions that seem irrational.*[13] The five fundamental premises of the systems-psychodynamic approach are summarized below.

The First Premise: The Influence of the Unconscious on Daily Life

Though hidden from rational thought, the human unconscious affects (and in some cases even dictates) conscious reality. People aren't always aware of *what* they are doing—particularly in the context of relationships—much less *why* they are doing it. Internal forces—feelings, fears, desires, and motives—lie outside of conscious awareness, but nevertheless, they are present in the form of "blind spots" that affect conscious reality and even physical well-being. These forces may be inaccessible within an individual to the extent that both *self* and *others* are blind to them, or they may be visible to *others*, but remain hidden to the *self*. Blind spots may be glimpsed in archetypal imagery that reveals the deepest levels of the psyche, where fantasy comingles with the "truth" of the world that is accessible through consciousness.

The Second Premise: We Are All Products of Our Past

Human development is an intrapersonal and interpersonal process. We are all products of our past experiences, including those from early childhood.

As adults, these experiences remain in the form of engrained patterns of behavior, although we are not always consciously aware of them. These patterns influence many aspects of life, such the way we form relationships, or the way we defend our personal values and beliefs.

The Third Premise: We Are All Regulated by Emotions

Nothing is more central to who a person is than the way he or she regulates and expresses emotions. Emotions color experiences with related (transferential) positive and negative connotations. Emotions also form the basis for the internalization of mental representations of the self and others. As a whole, therefore, emotions—in terms of regulation or expression—influence behavior and choices.

The Fourth Premise: Groups and Individual Dynamics Are Interrelated

Groups are subject to dynamics that arise from a collective of individual needs and motivators. These out-of-awareness dynamics arise from intrapersonal forces (existing within an individual, including past experiences, blind spots, emotions, and attachment patterns), as well as interpersonal forces (existing between or among people, including dynamics such as collusion and task orientation). Over the lifetime of a group, the intrapersonal and interpersonal forces will continually interact, and as a result will influence emotions and behaviors.

The Fifth Premise: Systems Are Also Subject to Unconscious Dynamics

Human behavior may be considered as a symptom, as well as a cause, of systems dynamics. All systems—which include by definition *organization* systems—are subject to irrational forces and may have their own blind spots. The system exhibits, and may act according to, the unconscious needs of its members.

To sum up, the conceptual framework of the broadly integrative systems-psychodynamic perspective offers a practical way of uncovering additional data about how leaders and organizations function: (a) from the psychodynamic or inside-out position,[14] (b) within the "middle" position of groups or teams,[15] and (c) from the outside-in, or systems, position.[16] As an applied methodology, the systems-psychodynamic epistemology "does not call for an abandonment of other organizational theories, but in many instances it supplements, qualifies, modifies, deepens, tests, and queries their arguments."[17] The systems-psychodynamic approach demonstrates more effectively than other conceptual frameworks that individuals are complex, unique, and paradoxical beings who differ in their motivational patterns. At the same time, this approach places human behavior in a relationship with the context in which it arises.

From the systems-psychodynamic viewpoint, organizations can be considered as systems that are "constructed, lived, and managed by individuals, each of whom has specific capacities and a specific unconscious."[18] Therefore, picking up a systems-psychodynamic lens helps us understand how the internal forces within one individual (the leader, or any other person) can ripple across to the edge of the organization. It also helps us to see how the ecosystem of the organization can seep into and color the psyche of the individual. In particular, this stance allows us to interpret what might appear to be human weakness as, in fact, a different form of rational behavior. Notably, the forces at play behind "irrational resistance to change or the incapacity to react in a crisis situation" become more visible.[19]

The Structure and Organization of This Book

We set the stage with the story of an organization—a system—in a "slow motion" crisis. In the next chapter, we go deep into the emotional heart of an organization in transformation. Next, we move to the middle ground, exploring the interrelatedness of individual leaders and the people around them. In a nuanced and counterintuitive approach, we present multifaceted stories of how toxic leadership arises from, and may be the cause of, crises in organizations. In the final chapter, we bring the focus to the intrapersonal level of systems-psychodynamics. As a way forward, this chapter shares a process for opening a reflective space that supports personal adaptability and recovery from crisis and change.

Two System-Level Chapters: Organizational Blind Spots and Idealization

Psychodynamic perspectives can be applied, by analogy, to organization systems: just as every neurotic symptom has an explanatory history, so has every organizational act; just as symptoms and dreams can be viewed as signs replete with meaning, so can specific acts, statements, and decisions in the boardroom. Organizations can develop blind spots; they can foster or deny collective memories.[20]

From a systems point of view, the repetition of certain phenomena in the workplace suggests the existence of specific motivational configurations. Organizational blind spots, for example, are described as mechanisms that enable organizations to remain committed to unworkable strategies. The formation of organizational blind spots is the result of a dual process: "fueled by unrealistic policies emerging in response to unconscious social demands, [...] blind spots are enabled by defense mechanisms (for example, splitting, blaming, and idealization) that play a role in maintaining commitment to unsuccessful strategies."[21]

Organizational blind spots, by definition, are difficult to see. In Chapter 2, Theo van Iperen brings to light a challenge that frequently remains out-of-awareness in organizations: cumulative crisis. Abrupt, acute crises are painful, visible, and hard to ignore; they generate a focused and rapid response. However, a cumulative crisis develops more slowly, through self-inflicted, deteriorating, and unexplored underperformance, most frequently caused by a legacy of mismanagement and/or poor decision making.

Most crisis or change-oriented interventions are designed to meet acute challenges and redress a threatening situation as quickly as possible. Strategy is developed and mandated at the top and cascaded down. However, van Iperen argues that managing a cumulative crisis requires a fundamental and holistic reorientation of the organization.[22] In his chapter, he deconstructs five cases of successful recovery from slow motion crises, among which the common denominator is an unusual bottom-up restructuring approach. He reports that further testing showed that the bottom-up approach is a valid model for developing a comprehensive corporate recovery strategy.

Chapter 3 takes us deeper into the secret life of organizations, complementing and developing our understanding of organizational blind spots. In "Reimagining Organizations: The Stories We Tell," James Hennessy recounts the emotional life—the memories and the fantasies—of a venerable, conservative organization that must come to terms with its past while environmental forces propel it into the future.

Hennessy demonstrates that while we do not usually think of organizations as generators and repositories of profound remembrance and longing, paying close attention to nostalgia and postalgia is also a valid method for understanding the existing state of an organization. Nostalgia and postalgia are usually thought of as being related to the way a person perceives the present as being unsatisfactory when compared with an idealized past or future. In psychological terms, such idealization can be employed as an anxiety coping mechanism.[23] This involves the attribution of inordinately positive qualities to things—such as memories, future visions, situations, or people—which actually house hidden anxiety.

Asking questions about nostalgia and postalgia, Hennessy provides a tremendous amount of data about employees' perceptions and feelings. In particular, crises can generate a particular mode of idealization called "chosen glory" within organizations. This refers to a shared mental and emotional representation of an event perceived as a triumph over adversaries or a calamity. The story is repeatedly cited to bolster a group's self-esteem, becoming part of an organization's identity, and passed on to succeeding generations of employees.[24] There may be little interest within the organization in considering the entirety of its actions with respect to past crises—for instance, how the organizational system itself might have, in fact, contributed not only to their "glorious" resolutions but also to the creation of the original challenge. In periods of disruption, Hennessy concludes, idealization of past and future, housed in influential organizational stories, is of great significance.

Two Group-Level Chapters: Perpetrators and Victims

Systems-psychodynamic theories related to group dynamics bring us to a tighter focus on the middle ground in organizations. The key concepts here add an *interpersonal* frame to the *systems* dynamics outlined in the previous chapters. Focusing analysis at the group level, it becomes apparent that behavioral patterns may also arise from the collective unconscious of the group itself, as well as from the individuals of which the group is composed.

Organizations are collections of relationships in smaller, formal or informal groups, in which visible or hidden group dynamics are always in play. From this perspective, human behavior—individually and collectively—is seen as a symptom, as well as a cause, of organizational dynamics. "Although the vector of influence goes from the system to the individual, the latter is never passively molded by impersonal collective pressures. On the contrary, [...] individuals often collude in creating them and keeping them in place."[25] This is how toxic leader–follower situations are formed, denied, or tolerated—and exacerbated in times of stress and crisis.

For example, while retaining a cognitive focus on change objectives, a leader may miss or ignore the emotional suffering of individuals, or of teams, or (last but not least) himself or herself. When group leader's silence, passivity, or lack of response is a result of his or her own emotional paralysis or uncontrollable anxiety, this is likely to aggravate the group's emotional distress. Group interactions may become flooded with overwhelming emotion; attempts at survival will replace constructive progress.[26] Everyone feels the resonance of suffering, but it is difficult to articulate, partly because it seems impossible to resolve.

As a consequence, particularly in times of crisis, people may unconsciously engage in destructive relationship behaviors in an attempt to reduce chaos and stress. Paradoxically, toxic leader–follower relationships may develop and even be perceived as normal. Three typical dysfunctional leader–follower relationship patterns are narcissistic leadership, identification with the aggressor, and folie à deux.

Narcissism can be labeled as either constructive or reactive, with *excess* narcissism generally falling in the latter category and a healthy degree of narcissism generally falling in the former.[27] Constructive narcissists tend to be relatively well balanced; they have vitality and sense of self-esteem, capacity for introspection, and empathy, while reactive narcissistic leaders become fixated on issues of power, status, prestige, and superiority. The result is that disposition and position work together to wreak havoc on reality testing, and the boundaries that define normal work processes disappear.

Healthy narcissism is a good thing in a leader. It underlies the leader's conviction about the righteousness of his or her cause and position. Such a leader inspires loyalty and group identification. Although it can be a key ingredient for driving change, narcissism can also become a toxic drug.

When a leader is perceived to have the power to inflict mental and physical pain, some followers may resort to the defensive process known as "identification with the aggressor." To protect themselves against possible aggression, they unconsciously mimic the aggressor's behavior, transforming themselves from "those threatened" to "those making threats."[28] Inadvertently, they may share the leader's eventual guilt about actions taken—guilt that can be exculpated through designating "villains" or scapegoats on which to project everything the group is afraid of.

Taken even further, some leader–follower collusions can be described as "folie à deux," or shared madness, a form of mental contagion.[29] In this case, a leader's delusions—for example, denial of a crisis or flight into manic activity—become incorporated and shared by other healthier members of the organization.

Collusive leader–follower relationships like these, with their induced lack of reality testing, can have various outcomes. In extreme cases, the outcomes of narcissism, identification with the aggressor, or folie à deux can lead to the self-destruction of the leader and the demise of the organization. The implications of the dark sides of leadership and followership may be amplified in a situation of crisis and change. No leader is immune from taking actions with destructive consequences and no follower from being an active participant in the process.

In Chapter 4, Fernanda Pomin addresses the topic of toxic leadership and the complexity of corporate leader–follower relationships. Narcissistic leadership, a topic that was until recently taboo and is still little understood, was the focus of her research. As a specialist in leadership development, she has encountered narcissists and witnessed the damage they leave in their wake. She also knows that many people in an organization see only the advantages of narcissistic leaders. In her study, rather than diagnosing the problem or vilifying the narcissist, she takes an unusual, systems-psychodynamic entry point: the experience of subordinates who perceive their bosses as narcissists.

Her research suggests a path to recovering a sense of agency for subordinates in this situation, including alternative strategies of control and influence over their own professional context. She also reminds us that although narcissists may appear confident and powerful, they may be struggling with low self-esteem and vulnerability themselves. Wisely, she advises us not to shy away from our own dark side—to seek within ourselves the seeds of narcissistic behavior, for better or for worse.

In a juxtaposition of perspectives with Pomin's research, in Chapter 5, Ross Emerson examines how the challenges of crisis and change may impact the well-being of leaders. In particular, he considers how top executives may be vilified, with blame and scapegoating cast upon a named individual, rather than on the function or the role. When the leader becomes the focal point for all the rage and distress that the greater context has unleashed, little consideration is given to the impact on that person. In his chapter, Emerson asks: "What happens to leaders— at the conscious and unconscious levels—when they are vilified?" The *perception* of being vilified—irrespective of actual behavior—can bring shame, trauma, and emotional scarring. Without pronouncing judgment, Emerson brings to the fore the importance of identity restructuring: a process through which an individual can reappraise, recreate, and move on—another form of individual agency and sensemaking.

A Final Intrapersonal Chapter: Know Thyself

The depth of the effect on senior leaders in the face of crises and change may not be fully understood for people who have not experienced the turmoil of organizational life. In Chapter 6, Ricardo Senerman writes from his own experience as a CEO and board member of several organizations. He has a public presence, feels public scrutiny, and is not immune to the stress and anxiety that comes with these positions. He wondered if a combination of methods for stress management and well-being might work as a simple but effective form of self-therapy for busy executives. Would he find some measurable sense of relief in stress symptoms, and meaningful insights about his own inner life? He settled on a study of *interoception*—the messages that the body sends related to emotions, such as sweating when you are nervous—and expressive writing (EW).

Senerman reminds us that all of us are aware of some of our thoughts and feelings, but a vast, unconscious part of our emotions and impulses remain out-of-awareness, blocked by our own anxiety and defenses. And yet, emotions remain influential, and as Senerman shows, they may be accessed and explored. In his action research study, Senerman developed a process for self-reflection that he tested on himself, experiencing and recording the merits and difficulty of a deep dive into one's own psyche. He writes, "a soft, clear conversation among several parts of me and even others started to take place."

Senerman's work is aligned with the intrapersonal field within the systems-psychodynamics. The intrapersonal encompasses everything which is inside us, known or unknown. Our inner life may appear in patterns of behavior or articulated through somatic symptoms or emotions.

One of the core concepts of the psychodynamic paradigm considers these patterns of behavior to be related to an individual's "inner theater."[30] Each one of us has an inner theater filled with people who have influenced, for better or worse, our experiences in life. These early experiences contribute to the creation of response patterns that in turn result in a tendency to repeat certain behavior patterns in other contexts, with different people. Though we are generally unaware of experiencing "transference"—the term given by psychologists to this confusion in time and place—we may sometimes relate to others as we once did to early caretakers or other important figures.[31]

The basic "script" of a person's inner theater is determined by the way the inner theater evolves through developmental processes.[32] A key concept here—containment—relates to the ability of the caretakers to provide good-enough presence. Good-enough containment does not prevent all frustration and fear, but it does help the baby (and later, the adult) to accept and tolerate ambiguity and anxiety.

Within the inner theater, certain themes develop over time—themes that reflect the pre-eminence of certain inner wishes that contribute to our unique personality style. These "core conflictual relationship themes" (CCRTs) translate into consistent patterns by which we relate to others.[33] Put another way, our early experiences and basic wishes color our life scripts, which in turn shape our relationships with others, determining the way we believe others will react to us and the way we react to others.

We take these fundamental wishes—our CCRTs—into the context of our workplace relationships. We project our wishes on others and, based on those wishes, rightly or wrongly anticipate how others will react to us; then we react not to their *actual* reactions but to their reactions as we *perceive or interpret* them. ("I suspected he didn't like me, and sure enough, his actions show I was right.") Unfortunately, the life scripts drawn up in childhood on the basis of our CCRTs often become ineffective in adult situations if we are not aware of them. The desire to develop self-awareness, as Senerman shows us, brings with it a certain degree of agency in how to act.

"If You Are Afraid of the Dark, Turn on a Light"

When conditions are stable in organizations, the saying goes: "statistics are enough." However, a purely rational-structural way of looking at organizations has never been a sufficient framework for understanding change in organizations. When everything goes crazy, we need the hidden data that the systems-psychodynamic lens reveals. The field of organizational studies is warming toward an appreciation of the contribution of the systems-psychodynamic approach to understanding crisis and change in the literature streams of leadership, critical management, change management, and organization behavior.

Unfortunately, this approach is often viewed by executives as something that appears glorious in theory, but impossible (and dangerous) to engage within the real world. For many leaders and observers of organizational life, the only thing that matters is what we see and know—in other words, what is tangible and measurable. It becomes downright frightening when the change spotlight is turned on the executives themselves, and they become aware of their own lived experience. Psychological defenses such as denial—at the individual, group, or system level—are there for a valid reason. They protect. But what is excluded from conscious awareness has, paradoxically, the strongest effect on behavior. In addition, whether we admit it or not, we take it all—emotions, transference reactions, and out-of-awareness blind spots—with us to work.

Our purpose with this book is to show that leaders and follow-ers in organizations can effectively manage adversity by tapping into systems-psychodynamic concepts, in ways that are pragmatic and applicable. The chapter authors bring us much richer and deeper insights into the "why" behind thorny organizational dilemmas. In the end, they show us that, if we explore the "why," we can at last advance toward "how": pragmatic and sustainable options for change.

Businesspeople can indeed conduct systems-psychodynamic research and also put this approach into practice in organizations. All of the chapter authors are not only senior executives or organizational consultants but also graduates (with distinction) of INSEAD's Executive Master in Change (EMC) program. The chapters are drawn from their original MA thesis research. The contributors provide us with real gifts: insights and renewed energy to change the way we live in the world of work.

CHAPTER 2

Back on Track

A Systems-Psychodynamic Approach to the Recovery of Organizations After a Crisis

Theo van Iperen

The Starting Point

Organizational crises are a dominant cause of a great deal of pain and stress in organizational lives. Taking the existence of such crises as a given, I am concerned with organizational recovery after a crisis. Most of the literature on organizational crises concentrates on unexpected, nonroutine events. This contribution, however, concentrates on organizational crises in slow motion: self-inflicted and deteriorating underperformance, most frequently caused by a legacy of mismanagement and/or poor decision making, which has come to threaten an organization's very existence. The question here is how best to recover organizations who have slipped into this danger zone.

Idea in Brief

The most common reaction to an organizational crisis in slow motion is top-down reorganization and restructuring, often with the help of some management consultancy firm. This approach is based on the classical economic perspective to organizations, but by far not predictive of success. This paradigm assumes that people are driven by rational calculation of their self-interest. This should require top-down leadership to drive recovery, as the change it demands triggers resistance among staff. Observing so many failures in organizational recovery based on this theorem, the question asked is whether approaches based on systems-psychodynamic concepts are better suited for sustainable organizational recovery.

Idea in Practice

The conclusion reached here is that to recover organizations from slow-motion meltdowns, a bottom-up recovery process that involves significant participation from an organization's own staff is the best way forward. This should be facilitated by frank and honest communication, building a holding environment, and creating urgency at the same time. An organization's operational processes should be central in the recovery process, without focusing too much on strategy, corporate structure, or culture. These efforts should all be supplemented with concrete investment initiatives building a clear prospect of the future prosperity of the organization. Together with fresh "holistic" leadership and a comprehensive change design, this proves the best way forward for the recovery of organizations.

Introduction

Because the life span of organizations is decreasing,[1] comprehensive organizational crises are likely to strike every generation of leaders and employees in an organization. As real change only begins and is accepted after an organization experiences real pain,[2] a crisis is a unique opportunity for fundamental organizational change.[3] The combination of crises' inevitability and their opportunity value makes their in-depth study both meaningful and apposite.

Method

To examine the question of how best to recover organizations from a crisis in slow motion, I review five iconic case studies of corporate revival to build a framework for recovery. To test this framework, I turn to related systems-psychodynamic approaches and leadership literature. I further test this framework by applying it to a study of ABN AMRO Bank that I conducted, before drawing several conclusions. As I will discuss, this case to a large extent supports the systems-psychodynamic framework for recovery I have developed.

The value of systems-psychodynamics in the case of crisis recovery is in the capturing of an organization's hidden undercurrents, which affect and drive human behavior, leadership, and decision making. As a crisis triggers all kinds of emotions within and between people in an organization,[4] sensibly studying this phenomenon is difficult without taking the systems-psychodynamic approach.

Organizational Crises

Most scholars of organizational crisis draw from C.F. Hermann's definition of a crisis from 1969, as "a situation that threatens high-priority goals ... which suddenly occurs with little or no response time available."[5] This starting point is built upon in more fulsome definitions of a crisis as a "low-probability, high-impact event that threatens the viability of the organization and is characterized by ambiguity of cause, effect, and means of resolution, as well as by belief that decisions must be made swiftly."[6] Crisis management may be defined as the "systematic attempt by organizational members with external stakeholders to avert crises or effectively manage those that occur."[7]

My concern with organizational crisis is not, however, the sudden unexpected accident, but the self-inflicted slow-motion meltdown caused by a legacy of mismanagement and/or poor decision making. Only rather recently has this type of crisis been recognized in crisis management theory. Hwang and Lichtenthal coined this a "cumulative crisis" and contrast it to the sudden unexpected crises, which they term an "abrupt crisis."[8] Their notion suggests that organizations are subject to two kinds of crisis: abrupt crises which come from swift forces that suddenly jolt organizations away from equilibrium, and cumulative crises which gather momentum slowly before breaking out. These differences have important implications for managing both kinds of crises. Where abrupt crises need a focused response, the cumulative crisis requires a fundamental and holistic reorientation of the organization.[9] Unfortunately, not much elaboration can be found on what such a fundamental and holistic reorientation should look like and how it has to be managed.

Building a Framework for Recovery

The most widely known and applied response to a cumulative crisis is the top-down reorganization or restructuring of an organization.[10] Beer and Nohria call this approach the Theory E strategy, where E stands for Economic value.[11] This theory is grounded in the economic assumption that people are driven by rational calculations of their self-interest. This assumption requires heroic leaders who forcefully manage programs of change down through an organization because change, as the disturbance of a static state, goes against the self-interest of people. No participation by an organization's staff is sought, as, from this perspective, people are not able to develop proposals or take decisions against their own interest.[12] The restructuring process is studiously prepared and planned in a programmatic manner, often with an extensive use of external business consultants.

The appeal of this kind of approach to organizations amid a crisis can be understood by the transformational object quality of heroic leaders and change programs, like the teddy bear is for a child leaving his or her parents for a night. As the system is in shock after a crisis, all-knowing heroic leadership, centralizing authority and delivering short-term solutions, comforts the organization and contains its collective stress.[13] Something similar occurs in the development of new organizational structures.[14] As a crisis threatens the existing structures,[15] the creation of new structures, which can be found in a meticulously designed change program, can replace the old ones and serve as new symbols of shelter and protection. We can expect that the call from the outside world—shareholders, authorities, public, consumers, labor unions, and press—will not greatly vary from the call for heroic leadership and top-down change from within. I call these dynamics the defense-mechanism trap. This pushes organizations toward the Theory E approach to fight a cumulative crisis, although case studies suggest this may not be the best way forward for organizational recovery, as the story of Air France shows.

Air France

When Bernard Attali took the helm at Air France, he found the organization in poor condition. To turn the tide, Attali hired the consultants of Arthur Andersen to put in place a plan to lower costs and increase productivity. As matters did not improve, Attali proposed further cuts—in the form of redundancies, a wage freeze, cancellation of destinations, and disposal of noncore activities. These proposals proved the trigger for the unions to call strikes, which ran out of hand and ended in violence, canceled flights, and runways blocked by burning tires. Under this pressure, the French government pulled its support for the plans and Attali resigned.

When Christian Blanc took over two days later, his first action was to reach out to his workforce. On his first morning in office, he went out to meet them in their own workplaces, starting with the most troublesome groups, explaining to them the state of the organization, assuring them he would start from scratch with making plans, and inviting them to share their ideas for recovery. He did the same toward the leaders of the unions that fought Attali. Over the next few months, he invited unions, management, and staff to share their analysis and suggestions for improvement. He surveyed the 40,000 employees of Air France on their grievances and solutions for the airline. Hundreds were interviewed face-to-face. Active communication was set up to share the findings of the surveys and the suggestions for improvement. Six months after his arrival, all 40,000 employees received the plan Blanc built based on the outcome of the surveys and interviews. Blanc made his own commitment to the plan clear by announcing his resignation if the plan was rejected. When a few days later the main labor unions indeed rejected the plan, he reached out to his staff again, by calling a vote. Eighty-four percent of them responded of which 81 percent voted in favor. Within three years, Air France was operating in profit again.[16]

This case suggests that it is not the traditional Theory E strategy that brings change to organizations after a cumulative crisis. From a systems-psychodynamic point of view, this is no surprise. Marks and De Meuse give an overview of the psychological and behavioral impact of this kind of transition, which ranges from a loss of confidence in management, heightened cynicism, and decreased morale to a lack of direction, risk avoidance, bureaucratic behavior, and the loss of team spirit.[17]

From this point onward, we can start building toward a comprehensive framework for organizational recovery from a cumulative crisis. To develop such a framework, it is important to first look at the common characteristics of cumulative crises. Subsequently, I investigate case descriptions of successful recovery processes in connection to systems-psychodynamic concepts in the field of change management and leadership in order to see what insights they can lend. This lays out a new framework for the recovery of organizations after cumulative crisis.

Common Characteristics

There is a wide spectrum of cumulative crises. What these crises have in common, first, is that they build-up slowly in an organization, gathering their own momentum until a certain threshold limit is reached.[18] Beyond that threshold, the organization tips into a crisis which plays out in the public domain and potentially threatens the existence of the organization. This process of degeneration makes the root cause of cumulative crises hard to detect. If such a cause exists, it may very well be disguised, potentially even as an abrupt crisis. This blurry origin can be seen as the second common dominator of cumulative crises. The third element is the impact it has on all the domains of the organizational system. The crisis does not concentrate or isolate itself in one element of the organization but spreads over the full community of the organization and its performance. The fourth shared element of cumulative crises is the impact they have on the psychology within the workforce, often expressed in terms of confusion, shock, stress, anxiety, anger, guilt, hopelessness, and despair.[19]

The broad impact of a cumulative crisis on the performance and psychology of an organization calls for fundamental organizational transformation.[20] This transformation should not only be limited to the technical/operational parts the system but should also include psychological/relational healing. This two-sided challenge is to be managed simultaneously if the organization is to be revived and experience posttraumatic growth.[21]

Iconic Recovery Cases

What lessons can we derive from case studies regarding successful recovery processes described in the available literature? For this purpose, I selected four other iconic recovery cases from business history. For a diverse selection in geography and public/private settings, I reviewed cases involving the New York Police Department, Philips (at that time one of the biggest electronic companies worldwide), Lufthansa (a German air carrier, state owned at that time, like Air France), and Nissan (the Japanese car manufacturer).

The NYPD[22]

Kim and Mauborgne refer to the practices of William Bratton, who served as commissioner of New York City Police Department (NYPD) in the 1990s, after a 20-year career as a police reformer in other parts of the United States. When he came into office at the NYPD, crime had gotten far out of control. Yet, in less than two years, Bratton turned New York into the safest large city in the nation. Based on an analysis of the five remarkable turnarounds he led, Kim and Mauborgne derive a four-step model to bring about rapid, dramatic, and lasting change to organizations.[23] The four steps are as follows:

1. Put managers face-to-face with the problems and with customers.
2. Focus on the hot spots and bargain with partner organizations.
3. Put the right people under a spotlight and frame the challenge to match the organization's various levels.
4. Identify and neutralize internal opponents; isolate external ones.

Philips[24]

About that same time, "Operation Centurion" led Philips out of a severe organizational crisis, after financial institutions had lost confidence in the organization and its share price had plunged. Despite the recession at that time, within five years, the recovery program raised revenues by

20 percent combined with a head count reduction of 15 percent, tripling the share price. Leading this process was Jan Timmer, Philips' CEO, supported by management guru C.K. Prahalad. The program taught Nigel Freeman, Philips' former Deputy Director of Training, the following "pillars" for dramatic change:[25]

- A comprehensive design of the change process, addressing both the emotional and the rational parts of the change cycle.
- Extensive communication, especially face-to-face in repeated large multilevel meetings, cascading down through the workplace to aid buy-in.
- The exchange of best practices and the willingness to listen to junior and younger people, creating a healthy environment for learning.
- Changing business and management practices through projects using stretched targets.
- A comprehensive, yet easily understood, model for steering the change process, combining both "hard" and "soft" outcomes.
- A variety of leadership styles to ensure that all aspects of the change process are covered appropriately.
- External support by outside consultants for worldwide facilitation.

Lufthansa[26]

While in the 1990s airlines worldwide gasped for breath, Lufthansa still survived, due to the unification of East and West Germany, which increased the number of domestic passengers. But the Gulf war also impacted Lufthansa, soon leaving it almost bankrupt. A few years later, under the leadership of Jürgen Weber, the company announced the best results in its history, becoming one of the most profitable airlines and leading partner in the Star Alliance network. From this history, Bruch and

Sattelberger, the latter a HR executive at Lufthansa during the transformation, derived the following lessons:[27]

- In dealing with a crisis, rely on one's own strengths instead of consultants.
- Provide space for reflection and dialogue by involving people in strategic business processes and creating a culture of openness.
- Foster intensive personal learning by top management.
- Build networks of change actors for systematic, institutionalized renewal, and invest in the bonding of the change actors.
- Irrespective of the crisis, create slack for continuous investments in strategically important resources.
- Create sustainable relationships with internal and external stakeholders for building consensus and support.
- Create clearly defined, durable platforms for the expression of emotions and practice of reflection within the workforce.

Nissan[28]

Before Renault announced its cash injection of $5.4 billion into Nissan, no other carmaker dared to touch Nissan. It had posted losses in six of the previous seven years, with only 4 out of 43 models profitable. Interest payments pushed out R&D investments. Renault's credibility as a rescuer was weak after its botched merger with Volvo. Cultural incompatibilities seemed to make a clash between France and Japan inevitable. But the miracle occurred: within three years, Nissan returned to profitability and recaptured consumers' faith. Quy Huy identifies the following as the distinctive success factors of this recovery case:[29]

- Nourish open communication with the workforce to get a good sense of the "smell of the place" and to build trust and alliances.
- Undertake actions and gestures showing respect to the legacy of the organization.

- Build up urgency by being repeatedly clear about the situation the organization is in.
- Create a safe environment and opportunities for anyone who is supporting the recovery process.
- Show daily determination to reach the goals of the recovery process.
- Mobilize staff to generate ideas for change, with change teams drawing from younger talent.
- Create an open atmosphere where everything can be discussed and only verifiable arguments are accepted.
- Create hope by giving room to new initiatives and investments in R&D, business, and product development.
- Align the compensation plans and other incentives with the new strategy of the organization.
- Be uncompromising and precise in the execution and monitoring of the recovery plan and its results.

Salient Similarities

Looking at these successful recoveries, including Air France, some striking similarities emerge. Table 2.1 summarizes the characteristics of each recovery story regarding specific recovery elements.

Although every recovery story has its own characteristics, there are some interesting shared elements in these stories. Turning first to the process elements. Though most of the recovery processes were involved with serious layoffs and terminations, no serious social unrest was reported in any of the cases. Presumably, the combination of building urgency, a broad consultation with staff, and the bottom-up development of the recovery plans contributed to this result. This is noteworthy, especially considering the centralized decision making and strong labor union presence in all these cases.

Another important element in these cases is the lack of management consultants driving the recovery process. At Lufthansa, this was notably seen as one of the success factors.[30] Even at Philips, the external management consultants did not take over the problems by developing

Table 2.1 **Summary of characteristics of displayed successful** *recovery cases*

	NYPD	Philips	Lufthansa	Nissan	Air France
Serious layoffs/termi-nations	—	++	++	++	++
Confrontation of the facts	++	++	++	++	++
Broad consultation of staff	++	++	++	++	++
Bottom-up plan development	++	++	+/–	++	++
Engaging middle management	++	++	++	++	++
Centralized decision making	++	+/–	++	++	++
Use of consultants	—	+/–	—	—	—
Large-scale commu-nication	++	++	++	++	++
New clear vision and values	+/–	++	+/–	+/–	+/–
Change of corporate structure	—	+/–	+/–	+/–	++
Acting on the corpo-rate culture	—	+/–	+/–	—	—
Acting on the daily operations	++	++	++	++	++
Projects as change drivers	++	++	++	++	++
Formal training programs	—	+/–	+/–	—	—
Investing in new opportunities	+/-	++	++	++	—
Scrupulous imple-mentation	++	++	++	++	

Legend: ++, very applicable; +/–, moderate applicable; —, nearly not to not applicable; blank, unknown.

the recovery plans, but mainly facilitated the process of recovery by moderating the hundreds of meetings, workshops, and off-site meetings that took place during the recovery process.

In terms of the content of these recovery cases, we see little effort placed on traditional recovery issues such as revising the strategy and reforming the organizational structure and culture. While typically chosen as starting points for transformation,[31] they are not mentioned in the case descriptions. Most attention was given to the improvement of daily operations, backed by a clear and determined vision on how to restore the organization, without necessarily spending time on strategy. A firm project-based approach to implement and monitor these improvements and keep staff and middle management accountable for the delivery of expected results underpinned all these efforts. Finally, despite the problems the organizations were in, they kept investing in new business opportunities.

Lessons From the Iconic Cases

Summarizing this analysis of the five successful recovery cases displayed here, we can distinguish the following common threads in these cases:

1. Establishing an extensive communication flow based on face-to-face communication: top leadership themselves reach out to the workforce.
2. Building urgency by confrontation with the facts and putting people face-to-face with the problems.
3. Creating a "holding environment" through an open environment for reflection, discussion, and dialogue; respecting the past; and inviting also the nonusual suspects to speak out.
4. Working from a clear and determined vision of how to restore the organization, without losing time on strategy formulation.
5. Fostering political stability by close collaboration with employees' representatives, giving clarity about job prospects and back-ups for staff cuts.
6. Using a comprehensive change design, installing change teams, and creating a network of change actors for systematic renewal.
7. Bottom-up development of recovery plans focused on the improvement of day-to-day work and new ways of organizing.

8. Taking concrete investment initiatives for building a clear prospect of the future prosperity of the organization.
9. Uncompromising execution and monitoring of the progress and results of the change process on both "hard" and "soft" variables.

Theoretical Underpinning

These findings might be called remarkable, as from the dominant economic paradigm in business research and practice it is hard to explain the success of radical organizational change driven by bottom-up development of plans by the organization's own staff. This makes me turn to another model to find explanation for these findings: systems-psychodynamics, with its attention to the undercurrents in organizations. As this new approach still doesn't offer one comprehensive framework, I draw from three related systems-psychodynamic concepts. These are emotional capital, the relational system theory, and fair process, together covering the systems-psychodynamic concept (Chapter 1). Emotional capital relates to what is going on inside each individual; the relational systems theory to the processes within and between groups; fair process to the organizational system.

Emotional Capital

The radical change necessary to match the holistic reorientation necessary for organizational recovery demands a paradigm shift which triggers defense mechanisms and resistance within the organization.[32] Quy Huy stresses the importance of emotional capital to deal with resistance and sees such capital as a necessary condition for radical change.[33] Huy and Shipilov define emotional capital as the aggregate feelings of goodwill toward the company by its staff. Emotional capital can be built by the actions of the company's executives.[34] Others also emphasize the importance of managing the emotional capital of the organization over the course of radical change.[35] Such capital is obviously damaged in the wake of a crisis. The question is how it might be restored with a view to building support for the recovery strategy. An absence of support is often due to resistance, a state that is exacerbated when uncertainties and fears are not taken seriously by leadership.[36] According to Huy, these uncertainties and fears create their own barrier to successful strategy execution and need to be tackled. He distinguishes five basic fears, each with its own defense mechanism. Accompanying this taxonomy are five strategies, which he terms as the five levers of emotional capital.[37] These strategies should be applied in any comprehensive attempt to engineer radical change. The five fears, their defense mechanisms, barriers to change, and antidotes are shown in Table 2.2.

These levers of emotional capital have important implications for recovery management, particularly with respect to the leadership style, communication, and change approach required. These points are explored in the next section.

Table 2.2 *Summary of the five levers of emotional capital*

Fear	Defense mechanism	Barrier to change	Antidote
Skills and roles will no longer be valued	Rationalizing why change is not feasible	Low receptivity to effortful change: change is for others	Value the existing competences and make clear these will be valued in future
Less personal future well-being	Sabotage	More talk than action, then mis-aligned action	Create the feeling that today's actions will improve future life for employees and society
Failing to meet new higher goals attached to the recovery	Set easy targets	Complacency: we are good enough, low urgency	Create dissatis-faction with the current state by imagining a more meaningful future
Less meaningful future work	Follow routines, no creativity	Mechanistic action: low creativity, low adjustment	Connect the change to mean-ingful personal development
Personal harm when honest opinions and feel-ings are expressed	Sharing mainly good news	Mistrust and low sharing of useful and timely information	Create a holding environment where people feel safe expressing opinions and emotions

Relational System Theory

Kahn, Barton, and Fellows center on the impact of a crisis upon an organization's relational system. While traditional crisis management theory is concerned with distinctively operational matters, Kahn et al. pinpoint the rebalancing of the disrupted relational system as key and claim that if this is neglected dysfunctional patterns of behavior will continue to reinforce an organization's vulnerabilities and performance lags.[38] Four elements are core to their vision of the healthy transformation of relational systems:

1. Redefining the "boundaries" of the system—these are the rules governing who participates and how in the system—to create and clarify new healthy relationships within the system.
2. The processing of emotional experiences between an organization's staff. Sharing experiences enables people to digest and leave behind painful events.
3. The construction of meaning through the composition of new narratives to reframe the situation in which the organization is in, enabling staff to collaborate and organize effectively.
4. Envisioning and creating a new desirable future for the organization. Hope offers the possibility of recovery and transformation.

Key to this formulation is working groups within which staff figures out the way forward.[39] Challenging them to come up with ideas and solutions for the organization's problems can be the driver for organizational and personal healing. Leadership should be available as transformational objects to help staff to overcome its anxieties and fears.

Fair Process

The concept of fair process can help us to understand how to use the potency of employee working groups. Fair process is founded upon a few simple ideas. The first is that whenever people experience pain they are highly sensitive to the procedure in which decisions are reached. Second, people will be more committed to decisions if they believe the decision-making process was fair. And third, when people are involved, they are prepared to override their personal self-interest.[40]

There is a substantial body of evidence from social and organizational research underpinning the above tenets.[41] The implication of this in the organizational environment is that employees will commit to leadership decisions—even ones with which they disagree or that are against their own self-interest—if they believe that the process used to make that decision was fair.

Kim and Mauborgne see three largely recognized principles to underlie fair process:[42]

1. Engage people in the process, by inviting them to have their input and challenge one another's ideas.
2. Explain why certain difficult decisions have to be made.
3. Set clear expectations by being honest.

In practice, fair process requires an approach in which staff are highly involved, most often in working groups. Up front, clear, and honest communication about the situation of the organization is a prerequisite, as is clarity in respect to the targets that have to be met, and transparency in the way in which plans are to be judged and in the decision-making process.

Synthesis

When we confront the findings of our case studies of organizational recovery with the theories examined, what lessons can be drawn for the creation of a comprehensive recovery framework? Starting from the lessons of the following case studies, in Table 2.3, I look at their treatment in light of the systems-psychodynamic theories examined and assess resulting implications for leadership in practice.

From this collection of the nine lessons from our iconic recovery cases, all but one—uncompromising execution and monitoring—are greatly underpinned by the systems-psychodynamic concepts consulted. This is not unexpected. While the psychodynamic theory is concerned with human behavior and an organization's hidden undercurrents, the implementation of a monitoring system following the progress of a change program is much more obviously a "hard" change catalyst. Though overlooked by the systems-psychodynamic theory, it remains in practice indispensable for real change,[43] as the case studies show.

Table 2.3 Framework for recovery from cumulative crisis

Lessons from our iconic case studies	Grounding systems- psychodynamic theories	Implications for preferent leadership practice
1. Establishing an extensive and personal communi- cation flow	RS: Share experiences enabling digestion and moving on RS: Be available as a transference object	—Conscious communication, being visible, and available for the organization —Show personal involvement and commitment —Put in place an extensive communication structure
2. Building urgency by confrontation with the facts	EC: Create dissatisfac- tion with the current state FP: Explain why difficult decisions have to be made	—Be honest about the bad news that has to be digested —Set new high-performance standards —Be courageous, outgrowing the need to please others
3. Creating a holding environment for reflection, discus- sion, and dialogue	EC: Create a holding environment RS: Facilitate the pro- cessing of emotions RS: Allow for confronta- tion and clarification	—Reach out to people, being available as a transference object —Show respect for the past, preserving identity and self-esteem —Invite people to speak out, pro- tecting the voices of leadership and looking for voices from all corners of the organization —Show vulnerability, inviting people to speak out, protect, and encourage
4. Working from a clear and deter- mined vision	RS: Construction of meaning RS: Envisioning a desirable future	—Develop a simple and unam- biguous vision for renewal and the new desirable future —Appeal to the collective imag- ination when speaking about that vision
5. Fostering political stability and rest	FP: Set clear expecta- tions by being honest	—Be honest about the impact and pain to suffer through the recovery process —Position oneself in the political field of internal and external stakeholders

(Continued)

Table 2.3 (Continued)
Legend: EC, emotional capital theory; RS, relational system theory; FP, fair process theory.

Lessons from our iconic case studies	Grounding systems-psychodynamic theories	Implications for preferent leadership practice
6. Using a comprehensive change design	RS: Redefine the boundaries of the system FP: When in pain high sensitivity to decision-making processes	—Develop and maintain a change program and structure —Set realistic but demanding standards —Create a wave of collective leadership, from different hierarchical levels
7. Bottom-up development of recovery plans	EC: Connect change to personal development EC: Value the existing competences RS: Install working groups RS: Participation opens up for successful change FP: People are committed to decisions if the process was fair	—Engage and inspire people to contribute to the restoration of the organization —Empower people to comply with the new expectations —Facilitate learning and development of capabilities —Provide focus and be goal and purpose oriented —Create an open and effective work group mentality and atmosphere
8. Taking concrete investment initiatives for the future	EC: Create the feeling that today's actions will improve future life RS: Construction of meaning	—Create an ambitious and appealing desirable future for the organization —Deliver the actions to foster these new ambitions —Help people to buy in to that new prospect
9. Uncompromising execution and monitoring	"Hard" technical and operational change processes to support soft change	—Be clear about expectations and rigorous in monitoring and rewarding —Implement a monitoring system to follow hard and soft change —Ensure compliance with targets

Leadership

Leadership in extreme contexts still remains a little researched area in leadership studies.[44] The analysis above includes several recommendations for leadership in times of organizational recovery after a cumulative crisis. Still, questions remain as to what leadership prototype is favorable for managing recovery after a cumulative crisis.

As leadership is key for the successful implementation of change,[45] a heavy responsibility rests upon an organization's top leadership during a crisis. The first and most urgent question to answer is whether or not incumbent leadership can take up this responsibility. There seems a strong case for new leadership after a cumulative crisis. First, while leaders seldom see themselves as part—let alone as cause—of the problems,[46] the personalities of top executives are probably a contributing cause of any crisis.[47] Second, as one of the challenges after a crisis is to change the imprint of the organization and bring it into new beginnings, it is doubtful whether the leadership under which a crisis has built up has the creativity and flexibility to pursue this urgent task. Given that decision makers display a strong bias toward perpetuating the status quo,[48] fresh leadership seems an inevitability. Research also suggests that new leadership is decisive for the success of the recovery process after a crisis.[49]

What awaits this new leadership taking the helm at the brink of a cumulative crisis? Probably, the first task is to contain anxiety without responding to the call for authoritarian, commanding top-down change.[50] Availability is important here so that leaders can become what we can call a transference object for the organization: an object to disassociate discomfort and project it onto.[51] To deal with denialism and other defense mechanisms, the leader has to create a holding environment which allows confrontation and clarification to overcome denial.[52] This means showing vulnerability, inviting people to share their anxieties and beliefs, protecting and encouraging dissonant voices, reframing situations to make them bearable, and creating hope and showing personal involvement.[53]

This is the psychodynamic "first aid" that a new leader has to apply. What follows this step is a process of structural psychological/relational healing and technical/operational restoration. The actions for psychological and relational healing relate to the emotional capital and relational concepts discussed earlier. The key capacity would appear to be deep felt belonging and empathy, authenticity, and sound intuition, all of which allow for the adaptation of the appropriate tone and actions.[54] For success, the leader has to have overcome his or her own anxieties and need for control, and recognize that others may be better at the job.[55] Self-awareness, without the need to impress or please, working in the moment, and being in tune with the bigger picture seem to be important characteristics for leaders in leading recovery.[56] Other qualities looked for are optimism, emotional intelligence, self-awareness, courage, determination, inspiration, protection, and compassion.[57]

For the operational recovery challenges, the psychological/relational healing must be combined with a complex responsive process, which meets the context of the organization and combines different intervention techniques.[58] Here, we move toward the field of more classical change management theory. For the success of operational change, some appeal to the "hard" skills of leadership should also be made, like creating a change structure, engaging others in this process, setting realistic but demanding standards, providing focus, making people stick to these standards, implementing monitoring systems to map change, facilitating the learning and capability building, and putting up a communication structure.[59]

From the different leadership typologies discussed in leadership research,[60] what ideal type of leadership emerges from this sketch of essential leadership capacities in a crisis? From our analysis, it seems we should look at the right column in Table 2.4 for the overview of pairs of contrasting leadership styles to find our ideal leader for organizational recovery.

There is no shortage of evidence to underpin such a choice. In their study of change leaders, Higgs and Rowland found that facilitating and engaging leadership behavior has a positive impact on change than more directive and leader-centric behavior.[61] Consistent with these findings, other scholars found transformational leadership often positively related to successful change compared to more transactional styles.[62] And other studies can be mentioned here too.[63] This analysis of requirements brings us to leadership notions like adaptive, transformational, authentic, and inclusive leadership, what I would call "holistic" leadership.

Table 2.4 Common pairs of contrasting leadership styles

Task leader	Social leader
Transactional	Transformational
Command and control	Participative
Authority and control	Supportive and therapeutic
Leader centric	Facilitating and engaging

The Framework for Recovery

Based on this analysis, I have derived the following framework for organizational recovery after a cumulative crisis. This consists of nine lessons from the case studies mentioned previously, of which eight are positively underpinned by the systems-psychodynamic view and one, on implementation and monitoring, which rests upon more classical change management theories, and two lessons derived from the analysis of the required leadership to manage a recovery operation. This brings us the following framework for recovery:

1. Installing fresh mature leadership, starting by personally developing a concrete notion of the situation by spending ample time within the organization.
2. A "holistic" leadership style, combining the authenticity, intuition, empathy, and professional will to inspire recovery.
3. Establishing an extensive communication flow based on personal and straight communication: top leadership themselves reach out to the workforce.
4. Building urgency through confrontation with the facts and putting people face-to-face with the organization's problems.
5. Creating a holding environment through the fostering of an atmosphere of open reflection, discussion and dialogue, respecting the past, and inviting the nonusual suspects to speak out.
6. Working from a clear and determined vision of how the organization can be restored, without losing time on formal strategy formulation.
7. Engineering political stability through close collaboration with employees' representatives, giving clarity about job prospects and compensation packages for staff cuts.

8. Using a comprehensive change design, installing change teams, and creating a network of change actors for systematic renewal.
9. Bottom-up development of recovery plans focused on the improvement of day-to-day work and new ways of organizing.
10. Taking concrete investment initiatives for building a clear perspective on the future prosperity of the organization.
11. Uncompromising execution and monitoring of the progress and results of the change process in terms of both "hard" and "soft" variables.

I hold this framework to be tentative in that it still requires testing in different contexts. In the next section, I explain how I began the testing process.

Testing the Framework: ABN AMRO's Recovery

Until 2007, ABN AMRO was one of the largest Dutch banks, with approximately 110,000 employees, 4,500 offices, and a presence in 63 countries. Due to a legacy of mismanagement, poor decision making, and persistent underperformance in comparison to their peers, the bank came under attack from hedge funds in 2007 which triggered a process of looking for strategic partners. While leadership favored a merger with Barclays Bank, they were outbid by a consortium of Fortis, Royal Bank of Scotland (RBS), and Banco Santander. In late 2007, this bid was finalized, and the consortium started the break-up of ABN AMRO. With the advent of the financial crisis in 2008, the situation came under intense stress. Fortis attempted to sell its acquisition to boost its own solvency, yet no buyer could be found, and Fortis was driven into bankruptcy. In October 2008, the Dutch government nationalized the former Dutch part of ABN AMRO together with the Dutch branch of Fortis.[64]

In December 2008, Gerrit Zalm, a former Dutch Minister of Finance for 12 years, was appointed as CEO of the new bank. His challenge was intense as the roller coaster of events had significantly impacted staff morale and the financial crises had damaged financial performance. The dismembering of the original bank with RBS and Banco Santander was still ongoing, and the integration between ABN AMRO Netherlands and Fortis Netherlands was emergent, with the patches of banks he was to lead amounting to approximately 35,000 employees.

The leadership of Gerrit Zalm spanned from December 2008 to December 2016. During this time, employee engagement consistently improved as did financial performance. In November 2015, the Dutch government relisted the bank by selling 20 percent of its shares to the public through an IPO. At the end of 2016, ABN AMRO's workforce had dropped to 25,000; 5,000 of these were stationed outside the Netherlands and the bank retained offices in 15 countries.

For this reconstruction, I conducted interviews with several executives and staff members closely involved in the recovery process. They came from different parts of the bank and worked at different levels. One of them was Zalm himself and one was a representative of the Workers Council. Additionally, I studied public material concerning the bank's recovery and the daily blogs by Zalm, bundled in eight booklets. All respondents received a draft version of this reconstruction, and their comments are reflected in the following text. Examining the ANB AMRO case according to each dimension of the recovery framework, I derived the following from the interviews and other materials.

1. *Installing fresh mature leadership, starting by personally developing a concrete notion of the situation by spending ample time within the organization*

   With the appointment of Gerrit Zalm, fresh mature leadership was installed, bringing 12 years of experience as the Minister of Finance to the table. Because he was unfamiliar with the banking profession, Zalm started with an extensive tour through the organization. Among parts of the top management, there was skepticism, as he wasn't a banker. In return, Zalm did not have warm feelings for the incumbent top management, who earned millions with the sale of the bank. The rank and file of the organization welcomed his arrival due to his high credibility. From the start, he began a daily blog with an average of 10,000 hits a day and invited people to reach out to him. This was appreciated as humane and transparent and created a lot of goodwill. The oppositional undercurrent in some parts of the top management did not lead to concrete obstruction but did hinder the cultural change of the organization for a long time. According to Zalm himself, leading a recovery process like this would not have been possible for anyone from inside the organization as being unencumbered is essential to build the necessary credibility.

2. *A "holistic" leadership style, combining the authenticity, intuition, empathy, and professional will to inspire recovery*

The appointment of Gerrit Zalm brought the welcome start of new leadership. By being available and approachable, Zalm broke with the more presumptuous style of the past. He was characterized as open, humble, empathetic and cohesive and at the same time persistent. A lot of the "old school" leadership disappeared on their own or at the bank's request in the first year after the nationalization. Zalm built his new team with people from outside and within. Still, his open style of leadership was not universally adopted by his fellow Board Members and beyond. A clear view of what the desirable leadership attributes were seemed to be missing and other, less open, behavior around him was too often tolerated. To the respondents participating in Top-100 leadership summits and trainings, a joint unifying leadership style did not materialize.

3. *Establishing an extensive communication flow based on face-to-face communication: top leadership themselves reach out to the workforce*

Zalm intentionally traveled a lot to the bank's branches to meet staff, speak to them face-to-face, keep an open nose for "the smell of the place," communicate the bank's recovery strategy and performance, and inform others about the sacrifices the organization and staff went through. He was transparent about staff cuts, helping people to understand the synergy impact as two organizations integrated. His honesty and openness in this respect was broadly recognized and appreciated and seen an important factor in managing people's emotions. He answered anyone's e-mails and was always available to visit an anniversary or reception when invited. This all resonated in a steady improvement of the employee engagement scores along the way. Though here too, respondents signal a lack of support from his fellow Board Members in this respect. With a single exception, no other Board Member followed his example of active and face-to-face appearance in the bank's branches, a lack that confirmed the old ways of doing business, workplace politics, and the importance of informal networks.

4. *Building urgency through confrontation with the facts and putting people face-to-face with the organization's problems*

The need to build up urgency seemed unnecessary, as the sequence of events in 2007 and 2008 made it already quite clear that urgency was required. These events were assessed to be sufficient by themselves to prepare minds for change, and the nationalization was experienced more as a relief than as a shock. Though seemingly no explicit strategy was executed in this regard, in his blogs, visits, and conversations, Gerrit Zalm often used metaphors to stress the urgency for change, one of which was that of an escalator going down while you want to go up. Others confirmed and praised the honesty Zalm displayed about the urgency to transform the bank and its impact.

5. *Creating a holding environment through the fostering of an atmosphere of open reflection, discussion, and dialogue; respecting the past; and inviting the nonusual suspects to speak out*

From the start, Zalm consciously worked to create an open environment, inviting people to speak out, protecting voices from below, and encouraging debate. His daily blog played a significant role in this effort and influenced the organizational culture. Thoughtfully, he used this medium to report on day-to-day meetings he had with rank-and-file staff members and to show what behavior he expected. He also hoped management would follow his example. He showed vulnerability by stressing his own limitations, apologizing for mistakes he had made, or showing a change of position due to information he had received from his conversation partners. As noted, the openness Zalm modeled was not adopted by most of his fellow Board Members. Such behavior was insufficiently corrected to reinforce a real change. Lower in the organization a great deal of time was taken to reflect and discuss the situation the bank was in, its causes, the culture, and the direction it had to take. During these sessions, questions were posed for the top leadership and answered soon after. This process was supported by daily Q&A sessions intended to inform staff and help them deal with their external stakeholders.

6. *Working from a clear and determined vision of how the organization can be restored, without losing time on formal strategy formulation*

The apparent need to rebuild the bank and his unfamiliarity with banking excused Gerrit Zalm from developing a strategy in the first year and a half, which had been pushed by some. Consequently, priority was given to the operational challenges of splitting and integrating different parts of the bank. As these were highly driven by compliance and external demands, there was no strong need to create focus with an explicit vision or strategy at that time. To comply with the expectations of the shareholder (the Dutch state) and prepare the bank for long-term relisting, Zalm choose to focus on cost savings and operational excellence. For his focus on the cost/income ratio, he introduced cost ceilings for each department. Later these orientations were combined in the concept of Customer Excellence, teaming Lean techniques with Customer Intimacy. The perceptions of this program differ. According to Zalm, the concept was developed and adopted bottom-up, others state that it was driven top-down through the organization. In the perception of most, the concept was contaminated because of the implicit cost reduction motive it incorporated, which prevented it being embraced. Nevertheless, the program contributed to the engagement of staff, supported transparency, and improved collaboration.

7. *Engineering political stability through close collaboration with employees' representatives, giving clarity about job prospects and back-ups for staff cuts*

The two Board Members, including Zalm, responsible for the relationships with the Work's Council, invested a lot of time and energy in managing this. This was recognized and appreciated by the Work's Council. In general, they were involved in decision-making processes early on in the process and were hence able to influence the outcomes of these processes. There were still occasions where decisions were made early by the Board, leaving the Work's Council to only join in execution. This situation worsened after the relisting of the bank at the stock exchange. The collaboration between the Work's Council and the Supervisory Board of ABN AMRO was important. As two Supervisory Board Members were appointed on behalf of the

Work's Council, they had regular access to that Board. This helped the employees' voice to be heard at all levels of the organization and gave comfort to the workforce, knowing that their interests were also being recognized there.

8. *Using a comprehensive change design, installing change teams, and creating a network of change actors for systematic renewal*
The breaking up of the organization and the integration of the remaining Dutch ABN AMRO and Fortis Nederland parts asked for a change design of military precision. Under the leadership of the COO, a robust transition organization had been installed, to manage these challenges. This is pictured as a parallel shadow organization. Tens of project groups were installed, robustly supported by an international management consultancy firm. This task was performed in isolation, as often their work was to be kept secret due to antitrust regulation, often literally behind locked doors. Terms used to describe this shadow organization were military precision, blind obedience, purely top-down, very programmatic, consultancy-driven, defined into the smallest detail, energizing, and tremendously powerful. Respondents were full of praise for this transformation process and its accomplishments.

9. *Bottom-up development of recovery plans focused on the improvement of day-to-day work and new ways of organizing*
The manner in which the transformation was managed was far from bottom-up as the picture of the transition organization shows. The same goes for the successive cost reduction operations. Though most respondents assessed this approach positively and believed it to be inevitable, it had downsides too. Several respondents refer to a disconnect between the parallel project organization and the line organization, which spread tension within the organization. This was partly due to the increasing role taken by external consultants which saw growing resistance. Information flows got stuck, as insecurity grew on how it would be processed. While to some it was always the line organization that had to comply to the project organization, to others the line organization often won the "game" as proposals from the project organization were frequently rejected. Although Gerrit Zalm himself downplays the use of consultants in this process,

others speak of an addiction to consultants with their high costs undermining the credibility of other cost reduction programs. The use of consultants lowered morale and self-esteem and was interpreted as a lack of faith in the internal workforce.

10. *Taking concrete investment initiatives for building a clear perspective on the future prosperity of the organization*

In the first years after the nationalization, no concrete initiatives were taken by the Board for new investment propositions to provide direction and s perspective on the future prosperity of the organization. These kinds of initiatives, which could have pictured the future ahead and built morale, were missed, but their absence is explained by the need for integration first and the market conditions of that time. Only after Zalm's initial years was more attention paid to initiatives that might build and modernize the bank's portfolio. The relisting of the bank was never considered to be used in this way. Though a landmark to many of ABN AMRO's employees, Zalm never used the relisting to drive action and morale, as he did not experience it as a big thing himself. When relisted, it surprised him how emotional this turned out to be for so many.

11. *Uncompromising execution and monitoring of the progress and results of the change process in terms of both "hard" and "soft" variables*

The execution and monitoring of programs like customer excellence, cost cutting programs, and the integration are characterized as vigorous, relentless, determined, disciplined, energizing, and compelling. Gerrit Zalm and his COO receive a lot of credit here, and their efforts are seen as a major contribution to the relisting of the bank. To monitor progress on the "soft" variables of the transformation, quarterly "mood reports" where produced. The idea of these reports was to enable management and staff to engage in talks on leadership style, behavior, and culture. In practice, these talks were not sustained, and the reports were abolished after only two years. Explanation for this is found in a rising confusion between means and cause: the discomfort the reports produced was blamed on the reports rather than creating awareness of the root causes underlying the anxieties the reports recorded.

Findings

What lessons can we derive from this case, both for ABN AMRO and from the theoretical perspective of the recovery framework developed in this chapter?

The following observations stand out in the ABN AMRO case. All respondents gave high praise of the way Gerrit Zalm and the transition team managed the recovery and laid out the foundations for the relisting. There is broad agreement that the personality of Zalm contributed importantly to this achievement. His empathy, perspective, humanity, and decisiveness are mentioned as crucial for managing the emotions during the recovery and keeping the bank together.

In hindsight, of course, some lessons can be taken from the recovery process. Though Zalm displayed the textbook "holistic" leadership style, this was not enough to nurture a more open and transformational culture throughout the organization. Divergent styles from other Board Members were not addressed and allowed the subsistence of an old-school leadership style deeper down in the organization. A missing common vision on the preferred leadership style and a resistance to addressing deviant leadership behavior were contributing factors here. The need for alignment among the top leadership team seems to be one of the key lessons from this case.

Though it appears there was no real reason for building up urgency, and that there was little space for initiatives envisioning a prosperous future, it may be assumed that more explicit attention here would have helped building up emotional capital in the organization. The fact that the relisting of the bank was so important to many and could easily have been used as a highly motivating goal looks like a missed opportunity here. It may also be the case that some ground may have been won by pushing the concept of Customer Excellence, which was eroded by the implicit cost reduction motives that stuck to it.

A final observation is related to the top-down and consultancy-driven approach driving change through a parallel project organization in which most of the change was managed during the recovery process. Though maybe partly inevitable due to antitrust regulations, it seems likely that ABN AMRO and its stakeholders, including the banking authorities, became victim here of the defense mechanism trap described earlier, choosing the "safe" way to change. Though the results seem positive, quite some tensions and downsides were signaled between the project organization and the line organization. While the suggestion that a more bottom-up, inclusive approach would have produced a better result remains speculative, the downsides of the chosen approach are clear in terms of tensions and decreased self-esteem. As other cases show, highly complex recovery processes can also be successfully managed in a bottom-up fashion. I regret that ABN AMRO did not grant its own people a wider role in the recovery process. The appeal which the fair process concept and relational system theory make on the part of staff engagement is too strong to be jettisoned on the basis of this case study. The evident tensions I recorded from the top-down and consultancy-driven approach show that a different process could potentially have been more productively implemented.

It is clear that a lot of the elements of the framework can be recognized in this case, and it thus offers support to the framework. The ABN AMRO-case confirms the following:

1. The necessity of fresh leadership
2. The leverage of "holistic" leadership
3. The importance of communication
4. The value of a holding environment
5. The notions about vision and strategy
6. The importance of political stability
7. The necessity of a comprehensive change design
8. The power of uncompromising execution and monitoring

While there are issues which this case does not transparently support—deliberately building up urgency, the bottom-up development of recovery plans, and the taking of future-oriented investments—they are not rejected either. On the contrary, there is evidence that such elements were missed by respondents and that their application could have benefitted the wider transformation.

One clear lesson for the framework for this case is that fresh leadership does not end with a new CEO, no matter how mature and "holistic" he or she may be. The full leadership team has to be engaged with that leadership style and trained, coached, and encouraged to act accordingly. The ABN AMRO experience suggests that leaders who cannot, or will not, follow might be best transferred from leadership roles to safeguard the integrity of the new leader and to foster the growth of a new culture. As leadership issues have recently resurfaced at ABN AMRO,[65] there are grounds for assuming that a more consistent execution of this aspect of change would have been of benefit.

Conclusions

This chapter plunged into the still little explored field of cumulative organizational crisis and related systems-psychodynamic concepts. Based on five iconic recovery cases, a first framework for the recovery of an organization after a cumulative crisis was derived. The common denominator of these cases was their taking of a transformational bottom-up character, rather than the more "classical" top-down restructuring approach. The underpinning of this framework was sought in several systems-psychodynamic concepts which confirmed the theoretical viability of the framework and added a call for a "holistic" leadership style in the face of recovery operations. Testing the model on the recovery of ABN AMRO confirmed its theoretical underpinning. This suggests that the framework is a valid model for developing a comprehensive recovery strategy, making it valuable for future substantive use.

CHAPTER 3

Reimagining Organizations

The Stories We Tell

James Hennessy

Introduction

I have spent nearly 30 years in a storied organization, one with a renowned history and replete with shared memories of the past and desires for the future. While we do not usually think of organizations in these terms—as generators and repositories of profound remembrance and longing—we nonetheless experience such feelings every day and reveal them in the stories we tell about the lives we lead at work.

My curiosity about these stories, and particularly my organization's past (hereafter referred to as the "Organization"), is what initially triggered my interest in nostalgia as a research topic; this later expanded to include postalgia, and the significance of both to the Organization's understanding of itself. This interest intensified as the Organization came under new leadership in 2018 and found itself to be in a stage of transition. Its future direction was unclear, causing considerable confusion within the Organization, and had potential consequences for its larger mission.

Nostalgia—a bittersweet longing for things from the past—is a feeling that exists in nearly all organizations. Its opposite, postalgia, a yearning for a bright future, is also widely evident in organizations as they discard the past in order to adapt to a changing world. Although they seem to relate to either the past or the future, both nostalgia and postalgia are actually responses to dissatisfactions with the present.

This chapter presents a case study that reveals the nature and effects of nostalgia and postalgia in the Organization. The research and findings are built on a series of socioanalytic interviews with individuals and focus groups. These interviewees consisted principally of a variety of employees of the Organization. I also interviewed several former employees who were identified as important "ghostly figures" whose influence within the organization continues to be felt. These former employees offered unique insights in reconciling the past and the future by respecting both: that is, appreciating and learning from the best of the past while recognizing that the future may require new approaches and attitudes.

The chapter begins with an overview of the key theoretical concepts of the case study and its methodology, followed by a description of 10 streams of nostalgic or postalgic feeling that emerged from the interviews. These streams carried the most fundamental concerns of organizational functioning and spirit. Nostalgic streams focused on vital matters such as the Organization's purpose and role, its understanding of leadership, and its conception of itself as a community. Postalgic streams expressed the desire for greater inspiration and a sense of belonging. Strikingly, postalgia is not much in evidence in the Organization, and the study suggests reasons why this may be so.

Applying concepts from systems-psychodynamics, which maintain that the most significant organizational difficulties usually include important, unstated emotional conflicts, I then focus on identifying several key emotional currents that underpin the 10 streams and reveal the possible interplay between nostalgia and postalgia. The chapter closes with the lessons learned from the study that can inform the Organization's decisions and actions as it seeks to move forward and the broader application of the study's methods and findings to other organizations. I was thus able to show how paying close attention to nostalgia and postalgia can help reveal an organization's existing and desired state, and may also be useful as an organization transitions to a new collective identity.

Nostalgia and Postalgia

Nostalgia is a universally experienced feeling, expressing an affection and longing for things from the past. It is felt by individuals and in organizations as they try to make sense of the world and construct their identities. Although it is commonly believed to relate to the past, nostalgia, in reality, is a reaction to the present. It expresses a discontent with current conditions or, more simply, a yearning for things that seem to have gone missing from life. The idealized memories of nostalgia are considered richer, more authentic, and meaningful than the present.[1]

Nostalgia is a mixed emotion, usually described as consisting of happy feelings of beauty, satisfaction, goodness, and love, yet also having a bittersweet quality. It almost never stems from experiences of upset, hate, or shame[2] nor unresolved trauma or psychic injury. At the same time, nostalgia always includes a pronounced element of loss related to the past, the absence of something that feels out of reach.[3] It is a joy tinged with sadness.

Although nostalgia always looks to the past, it is not actually a product of the past, but a reflection of present conditions. Nostalgia selectively takes memories and idealizes them, in effect creating fantasies of the past that are imbued with glowing emotion and symbolic meaning.[4] It uses these pleasing images to highlight what's missing or gone wrong in present times. It doesn't matter if the past was not, in fact, experienced as nostalgia now purports;[5] nostalgia has little to do with historical veracity. Rather, it is concerned with appealing, useful stories that are continuously revised "to match the mood of present times."[6] As University of Bath Professor Emeritus Yannis Gabriel maintains, nostalgia is not a way of coming to terms with the past, but an attempt to come to terms with the present. In this way, nostalgic recollections play a powerful role in how present-day events are felt and understood, both individually and in organizations.[7] It is one lens through which to make sense of life at work.

For many individuals, nostalgia provides protection from, and a cure for, the injuries to our narcissism inflicted by organizations. By their nature, modern corporations are impersonal and unemotional. Nostalgia seeks to return us to an imagined time when the organization was less bureaucratic and more like an extension of our own family, with ourselves uniquely at the center of a caring world.[8]

For groups, organizational nostalgia appears to serve multiple purposes. One foundational study has proposed that nostalgia is central to understanding the construction and maintenance of collective identity.[9] Groups come to define themselves through the creation and sharing of stories. Nostalgia significantly enriches the meaning of these narratives by helping the group to understand its present circumstances, preserve the self-esteem of group members, and provide a defense against perceived threats to group identity.

Nostalgia may not, however, always be experienced positively by individuals or organizations. If, for example, an organization faces unwelcome developments, nostalgia could prompt some of its members to react with psychodynamic defenses such as idealization, splitting, rationalization, and denial, in an attempt to shield themselves from the frightening possibilities or consequences of change.[10]

Organizational postalgia is a more recent concept, posited in 2004 by VU Amsterdam Professor Sierk Ybema. It can be defined as a longing for a bright, promising future. According to Ybema, this idealized future involves directive change and the abandonment of the past within the organization, and it is typically led by the managerial upper class responding to the demands of new operating environments, opportunities, and threats. Thus, like nostalgia, postalgia is primarily about dissatisfactions with the present, which, within organizations, animates the imperative to change.

Postalgia and nostalgia are alike in three key ways. Both compare the present with another time and find it unsatisfactory; both look to an idealized temporal realm as their lodestar; and both are attempts to come to terms with the present. But emotionally and functionally, postalgia and nostalgia seem to be very different. According to Ybema, managerial postalgia is an "activating force," while nostalgia is a slower, reactive response. Postalgic dreams are usually presented as rational, purposive plans for change, whereas nostalgia is commonly expressed through tales about "the good old days." They also differ in the underlying affective orientation they seem to generate. Despite its deliberate projections, postalgia can have a nervous, anticipatory quality, often swinging between extremes of pessimism and optimism.[11] Postalgia lacks nostalgia's settled consolation for fully realized life events. For, unlike an uncertain future, the past and its golden representations cannot be taken away.

Methodology

The methodology for the research was that of a case study, with aspects of ethnographic research. As a case study, it explored a phenomenon within a bounded, real-life organization, through the collection of detailed information from multiple sources.[12] As ethnography, it included qualitative description and interpretation of a group's values, behaviors, and language, and sought to discern patterns of social organization and belief systems.[13,14]

Data were gathered through socioanalytic interviewing (the "Conversations"), which aims to assemble data from multiple interviews to arrive at a full picture of an organization. Interviewees are provided a "space" to express their views, while the interviewer listens carefully for content, feelings, and signals of unconscious phenomena. Identifying these latter phenomena may help illuminate shrouded impulses that could significantly impact an organization's ability to do its work.[15]

The interviewees (the "Respondents") were all current and past employees of the Organization, with varying seniority and tenure, and who experienced the organization over different periods of time. In selecting Respondents for the study, the goal was to compile a valid set of emotionally rich sources of memories, anecdotes, dreams, and desires that would reveal various streams of nostalgia and postalgia in the Organization. Overall, I sought a mixture of men and women, from all levels, and from a variety of different business and support areas. I also sought a combination of those who had joined the organization before a major global crisis in 2008 to which the Organization responded and those who had joined after the crisis: I hypothesized that this distinction might have implications for nostalgic and postalgic feelings.

The 35 respondents fell into four cohorts (the "Cohorts"), corresponding to their rank or status within the Organization: 13 senior officers (the "Seniors"), 5 junior officers (the "Juniors"), 13 staffers who are nonofficers (the "Staffers"), and 4 "ghosts" (the "Ghosts")—former members of the organization, all of whom had been senior officers. The respondents' length of service varied from 2 to over 40 years. In January 2019, I interviewed the Seniors and the Ghosts individually. In early February, I conducted one focus group of Juniors and two of Staffers.

All Respondents but the Ghosts were asked before the interviews to consider the following two open-ended questions about nostalgia and postalgia in the Organization:

1. Thinking about the time you have spent within the organization, what memories bring warm longings for past times?
2. Envisioning your future time within the organization, what needs to be changed or abandoned? What new or different qualities or feelings do you find yourself wishing for?

The two questions posed to the Ghosts prior to their interviews were slightly different:

1. Thinking about the time you spent within the organization, what memories bring warm longings for past times?
2. In leaving the organization, what was your postalgic dream? What new or different qualities or feelings do you find yourself wishing for?

Asking about nostalgia and postalgia proved to be of unique value. The questions almost seemed to put people into a kind of dream state. This made their feelings much more accessible to them, and the resulting responses much richer than traditional data concerning organizational culture. Typical questions, such as directly asking, "What do you think of your organization?" can lead to discussions that are narrowly focused on immediate work issues and often devolve into gripe sessions. Asking instead, "What do you miss from the past and what do you fantasize for the future?" removed people from the present and had much more emotional resonance.

Streams of Nostalgia

The interviews revealed 10 primary streams of nostalgia and postalgia in the Organization. Seven streams of nostalgia related to purpose, role, leadership, community, rituals, intimacy, and anti-nostalgia. As already stated, the Organization finds it difficult to engage in postalgia, and the data indicated several reasons for this, including a lack of urgency, fear, pessimism, and avoidance. Three distinct streams of postalgia appeared in the data expressing a longing for inspiration, a desire for greater communal belonging, and one that conveyed an acute fear of future organizational irrelevance.

Stream 1: Purpose

The different streams of nostalgia in the Organization are intertwined, playing-off of, and reinforcing each other. But perhaps the deepest stream of nostalgia is a sense of purpose, which here ultimately means service to others. Respondents in all Cohorts spoke of purpose and service. A number of Staffers cited purpose as a motivating source of pride, and several stated that service to others was the reason they decided to join the Organization. But purpose and service were spoken of most ardently by the Seniors and Ghosts.

Purpose appears to be felt most powerfully during or in the wake of crises, creating a heightened "feeling of mission," as one Ghost put it, "and that we're all part of a team." Several other Respondents expressed the same sentiment. On one occasion, in the most extreme circumstances, according to one of the Ghosts, purpose in the Organization went beyond service to others, and became "sacrifice" for others. Strikingly, this incident of sacrifice was not business related, but happened during the course of the nearby 9/11 terrorist attack, during which the Organization took in the injured and others in need. This, the Ghost said, was the most poignant moment of his long career.

There was no conflict among the Respondents as to the purpose of the Organization. However, there was a definite feeling that it was less certain than a decade ago, perhaps because there had been no crisis during that period. There is quite evidently a nostalgic longing throughout the Organization for a stronger, clearer sense of purpose.

Stream 2: Role

The Organization's role is closely bound to its purpose. That role seems fundamentally to have changed since the turn of this century, provoking feelings of loss, bewilderment, and foreboding, especially among the Ghosts and Seniors. These changes and feelings were hardly mentioned by the Juniors and Staffers.

Historically, the issue of role has centered around the conviction that the Organization had a unique position within a system of similar, related organizations (the "System"). It was, one Ghost stated, "The first among equals."

This sense of uniqueness was a defining feature of the Organization's perception of its role until about 2005. According to the Ghosts and Seniors, its special qualities stemmed from two main elements—its unparalleled expertise and its drive to "do what was right." Its expertise was a function of the high quality of its people and, as one Senior put it, knowing "how the world actually works." "Doing what was right," as explained by another Senior, meant developing strongly held, independent views and, if necessary, pushing back in decisional matters that involved other players in the System. The Organization felt strong, semi-autonomous, and active during this time, which, the Ghosts and Seniors believe, enabled its work to "make a difference" and have "real impact" within a System that was "prone to rest."

During the last 15 years or so, a good deal of the perceived uniqueness of the Organization's role seems to have dissipated. This has been due, apparently, to a combination of factors. The Ghosts, in particular, point to neglect and a lack of belief and will on the part of its CEOs (the "Chiefs") that the Organization had, or should have, a unique role in the System. According to the nostalgic stories of the Ghosts and some of the Seniors, this has led the Organization to become weak, reactive, and preoccupied with "process" rather than, as before, its impact in the System and beyond.

Stream 3: Leadership

Surprisingly, nostalgia concerning leadership in the Organization focused almost exclusively on one former Chief, who left the Organization over 25 years ago. These feelings of admiration emanated from Ghosts and Seniors.

Uniquely, this Chief was described by Ghosts and Seniors as being deeply thoughtful, with a strategic vision that was able to "see around corners" and understand the external environment and oncoming trends. In terms of working style, the Chief was very "hands on," and thus connected with staff across the Organization, who felt his "care." The Chief "loved" the Organization, believed it was a "special place," and fostered "a family environment of sorts." This created what one Ghost called "a commitment chain" across the Organization. The Chief was also said to have had "courage." Nevertheless, several Respondents noted that the Chief had significant personal flaws.

Some of the Seniors also nostalgically cited some of the Ghosts as great leaders of the Organization. These Ghosts were said to have "really cared" for their people, they "had your back," and they were passionate.

However, one Senior warned against taking a nostalgic view of past leaders, saying that the Organization has a history of treating its leaders as "kind of royalty or heroic figures." And while not denying their significance, this attitude "radically simplifies" complex people and their actions. This Senior also believed that encouraging the idea of mythical figures can lead to dysfunction, such as the creation of silos and cultures of loyalty to individuals or groups, rather than to the Organization as a whole.

Nonetheless, one Senior lamented that there didn't seem to be any great figures in the Organization anymore. "They're all gone."

Stream 4: Community

Nostalgia for the Organization as a particular type of community—specifically, "being like a family"—and how that sense of community has changed and been lost over time, generated more discussion than any other topic. Respondents from every Cohort commented on it.

Since its inception, the Organization appears to have thought of itself as a kind of family. Seventy-five years ago, reported one Respondent, the employees even referred to it as "Mother Org." One Junior stated that the feeling of family came from two sources—the shared commitment to the Organization's mission, and the perception that it would "take care of you." As one Ghost put it, "Consciously or unconsciously, management understood that if they cared for their people, then their people would be loyal and deliver."

Many recalled the Organization's caring included not only an expectation of job security, but also "how people related to each other." One Ghost said that the "feeling of family" engendered trust, high morale, and an environment where people could "cohere and do their best work."

Several Seniors, who fondly remembered the Organization as more of a family, also highlighted some considerable downsides. "When people talk about family," said one, "it's code for bad management"—adding that this often meant that poor performers were shuffled around and that this fed the perception that there was dead weight among the employees. Other Seniors also recalled the old environment as extremely hierarchical and formal, with something like a caste system dividing managers and employees, and men and women.

Respondents reported that the "family" sensibility continued roughly until the early 2000s, when there was a series of downsizings. The relationship between management and staff began to change. One Ghost explained that staff came to be viewed by some senior leaders as "not part of the core" of the Organization—"They're not like us."

One Ghost framed these changes within the Organization in different terms. He explained that in the old days, "psychic income" was the most important form of compensation in the Organization—that is, people were motivated by being part of and making a contribution to something greater than themselves. According to the Ghost, this feeling had been lost as more tangible forms of compensation began to take precedence, and "people whose primary motive was service gradually shifted more toward self-interest."

Stream 5: Rituals

Connected to the community stream, but also to individual experiences, is nostalgia for rituals such as gatherings and observances—celebratory and serious. Notably, unlike most other streams of nostalgia, remembrances of rituals all included a prominent element of place.

Strong feelings about long-standing rituals were expressed by Respondents from all the Cohorts. Almost all of the discussions referred to recent attempts to create "more inclusive" rituals concerning the announcement of promotions, and the annual holiday party.

Many of the Seniors and Juniors regarded their elevations to officer rank as a signature event in their careers, describing it as "a really special experience," "exciting, meaningful," and a transition to becoming "an official representative of the Organization." All of them recalled "the steps of the day," culminating in being called over to the historic executive floor to be individually congratulated by the Chief. One Senior noted that, in comparison, all subsequent promotions fade into oblivion.

Many Seniors and Juniors also expressed nostalgia for the old holiday party, held in the Organization's formal dining room following the promotion announcements, which in the past had not included Staffers. One Junior commented that the old style of party fostered "camaraderie" and created new "relationships and communities" that were like "branches of a family." Still, their nostalgic feelings about it were more muted in comparison to the enthusiasm of the Staffers for now being included in a single, organizationwide event, marking promotions at every level. The old holiday party had been "really depressing and demoralizing," said one Staffer, whereas the new party was described as "spectacular, great." "Everyone was talking about it because it was so much more inclusive and jovial."

Stream 6: Intimacy

A number of Respondents shared stories of personal nostalgia related to their time in the Organization, recalling experiences with others or places that created a special feeling. I collected these under the heading of "intimacy," in the sense of close or affectionate relationships.

These experiences were almost exclusively the domain of the Seniors. For many of them, and in contrast to their current lives, their first few years in the Organization were characterized by feeling "more like a family," socializing with colleagues, and deep friendships. All are missed, though many accept this loss as a function of aging.

Nonetheless, one Senior made the case for deeper personal relationships at work. She maintained that people appreciate "the whole person" and work better together when they have stronger relationships, as they used to. Now, in contrast, "it's possible to work with people for years and literally know nothing about them."

Another Senior spoke warmly about places in the Organization's headquarters, some parts of which have been altered or lost over time. He missed the way the building used to look, with its "caverns and labyrinths," and in particular, a narrow old hallway that was removed during a renovation 10 years ago. "It echoed differently when you walked down it because it had a cork floor," this Senior recalled, "It felt intimate, like you were going somewhere different; that meant something."

Stream 7: Anti-Nostalgia

Along with the six streams of nostalgia discussed so far, there runs a related stream of anti-nostalgia in the Organization. It broadly articulates the harmful consequences of nostalgia across a range of issues and activities. The anti-nostalgia stream emanates almost entirely from the Staffers, along with a few Seniors.

These Respondents felt that there is too much nostalgia in the Organization, clearly expressed by one who said, "We have a surfeit of it here." One Senior went even further, positing that the Organization has "imagined nostalgia"—a yearning for something that never actually existed, but is believed to have gone away, and, if it could only return, would remedy some difficulty. This Senior cited the belief in the Organization's "independence" within its larger System as an example.

Staffers described how nostalgia often shuts down debate or creates a false sense of security. One Staffer stated that the invocation of "the good old days" is sometimes used as a justification, without explanation, for how things "get done" in the Organization. This turns "the way we have always done it" into a kind of "gospel," making it a "sin" to question it. Another Staffer recognized this scenario, adding that it is even worse if the process in question was implemented during the 2008 crisis; many ways of doing things, said this Staffer, have been held onto ever since. In addition, he said, while the response to that crisis demonstrated the dedication and passion of the employees, it also set unreasonable expectations for normal times—"anything under the Sun can get done in three days." This, in turn, feeds undue confidence in the Organization's ability to cope with a future crisis.

Streams of Postalgia

Stream 8: Inspiration

Members of all Cohorts concurred with a summary offered by a Senior that characterized the Organization as having "nostalgia for the past and muddling through the present." Several Juniors added that the Organization lacks clarity about what its future role will be and, as mentioned earlier, appears to be reactive. Staffers indicated that this contrasts starkly with their experience in other organizations, where "if you weren't moving forward, you were lagging behind" and that the Organization is missing "that ambition to get ahead of the next curve, before it's upon you." While some people genuinely pursue change, it is generally not encouraged, and overall "there's not much in terms of futurism." Instead, one Staffer recounted, the narrative is about the mission of the Organization and the pride and service of its employees—"end of story."

Several Seniors and Juniors suggested some possible steps toward developing a postalgic vision for the Organization. These involve granting "permission" to engage in postalgia along with understanding what a postalgic vision is not. Its leadership, advised one Senior, needs to signal that "it's okay to let go for a while and think about the future." A Junior agreed, stating, "I'd like us to be less operational, get our heads out of the books, and look into the future."

Numerous Respondents from all Cohorts called for a new, inspirational vision. The substance of this vision and how to arrive at it were described in various ways. One Senior suggested a collection of "four or five visionary strategic statements that would resonate and motivate." Two others, recalling their past experiences in the Organization, recommended a big, bold, outward-facing agenda. "We don't need a crisis," one of them said, "we should be working on problems before they happen. There's still plenty to do. How can we make the world a better place every five years?" She said that such an agenda must take the long view, be single-minded, and unafraid.

Most importantly, said several Respondents, the Organization would need to "paint a picture" of its vision. "The vision is the thing that makes me excited, is what invigorates me," enthused one Senior. But without a full picture, warned another, the vision will "just get questioned, and questioned, and questioned." Painting this picture is the primary job of the leadership of the Organization, maintained one Senior. "We have an absence of understanding of what a leader is: We don't have to communicate. We don't have to use colors. All we do is think. And we don't think we have to inspire."

Stream 9: Belonging

The postalgic stream of belonging addresses the kind of environment and rules of engagement that Respondents would like to see in the Organization. Four components—togetherness, acknowledgment, safety, and possibility—emerged from the interviews.

Togetherness, or the dream of unity, was mentioned in some form by Respondents from all of the Cohorts. Without characterizing the Organization as a family, there does continue to be a desire for a greater sense of togetherness, though its exact form and meaning remain unclear. For one Senior, it would mean "we're all part of it" and, consequently, there would be much less "us vs. them" in the Organization. Specifically, there would be less "old Org vs. new Org" or divisions between longtime employees and those of newer vintage. "I wish all that would go away," she said, "everybody has their stories." The Juniors also voiced a desire for "a shared vision" and to feel "less atomized and disconnected" from each other, and from the higher mission of the Organization.

Acknowledgment is a component of belonging that refers to a variety of ways for individuals to be valued for their unique contributions to the Organization, and to be heard, appreciated, and accepted as their true selves. One Senior spoke about the importance of differentiating among people according to whether they were good managers, excellent specialists, change agents, or flourished within defined structures. This recognizes individuals' strengths and makes them feel they have a place. Juniors and Staffers also weighed in, some expressing a desire for more outward recognition of their work and how it added to the overall mission of the Organization, and others endorsing the need to support the "whole authentic self" at work, so that everyone could "contribute and be their best."

The anti-nostalgia stream indicated that Staffers sometimes felt "shutdown" if they tried to raise questions. This phenomenon is part of a larger concern about *safety* in the Organization in a number of related respects—safety to speak, to be wrong, to learn, to disagree, and to surface unspoken conflict. Several Seniors articulated a wider unease in this regard. One noted that learning itself requires some sort of disruption and a feeling of cognitive dissonance—"of being a little lost"—which is difficult to accept and process unless there is an atmosphere of safety. Moreover, this Senior maintained, the Organization needs to find ways to have "good, stressful conversations" about disagreements and to acknowledge that there is often a great deal that remains below the surface, unspoken—"What could we do to confront this a little more honestly?"

Respondents also expressed a desire for a greater feeling of *possibility*, wanting more openness and optimism. A number of Seniors and Juniors indicated that they routinely observe outsized negativity, skepticism, and a paralyzing doubt—which leaves them feeling alienated from their colleagues and the work of the Organization. Part of the problem stems, according to one Senior, from the academic rationalism that dominates the Organization's mentality, with a culture that values experts, more than managers and facilitators. According to both Seniors and Juniors, this leads to the overanalysis of data and excessive faultfinding. One Junior noted, "Just once, I want to hear someone say: I'm sure we should do this. I have never heard anyone say, yes, I'm positive we should do this, this is the right thing to do."

Stream 10: Fear of Irrelevance

The final stream of postalgia is not a dream for the future but a nightmare about the Organization's possible future irrelevance. This concern was highlighted by a few Seniors, but it was expressed with particular alarm and emotional vehemence by the Juniors.

One Senior made the general case: "Dogmatic living in the past is profoundly unhealthy, and we must evolve over time. If we are not prepared to change, inevitably we're going to find ourselves irrelevant." In response to this threat, three Seniors proposed creating a special division devoted solely to looking to the future. "We have too many people who are enamored with blades of grass," commented one Senior. Added another, "We need people who are busy looking out ahead and around the corner." This unit would be a kind of SWAT team, identifying what is different in the environment, and asking questions about how new things work.

The Juniors identified the biggest threats to the Organization's relevance as changes in external operating models and developments in technology. One Junior explained, "We're a node in a larger financial system. And these days, something can just be like—boop!—the node is no longer needed. And no one is thinking about that." One Junior cited attempts, last year, to try to get the Organization to consider such threats and its future relevance, but to no avail. Instead, immediate worries remained the highest priorities. "We take our existence for granted and don't even want to see the risks that are out there, or be proactive." Another said, "We are totally blinded by the risk of being disintermediated within 10–15 years." And a third attributed this blindness to "the fragility we have about doing something wrong." As a result, he said, "We just can't get our heads around what issues might come to be. And the future is really close, if you think about time."

Psychodynamic Forces at Work

As described earlier, although nostalgia and postalgia are usually thought of as being related, respectively, to the past and the future, both in fact compare the present with another time and find it unsatisfactory. They offer idealized versions of their respective temporal realms in an attempt to come to terms with the present. In psychological terms, such idealization can be employed as an anxiety coping mechanism in which a subject of ambivalence is viewed with overly admirable qualities.[16] This involves the attribution of inordinately positive qualities to things—such as memories, future visions, situations, or people—which actually house hidden anxiety. Thus, idealization and its consequences are particularly relevant across this analysis, as manifested in several powerful psychodynamic forces evident in the Organization.

Splitting: The Idealization of Purpose and Role

Without question, the employees of the Organization are primarily, in my view, admirably motivated by service to others. They believe that the Organization has a meaningful impact on the world. As evident in both nostalgic and postalgic streams, they appear to long for a reaffirmation of this understanding of its purpose—service leading to external impact—and believe that this can be achieved through clarification of the Organization's role, and the articulation of a compelling vision by its leaders. Without such a vision, many Respondents fear that the Organization will eventually become irrelevant.

It is striking how uniformly the employees believe in and hold a positive opinion of the purpose of the Organization; not a single contrary or cynical view was expressed in the Conversations. This strongly suggests a good measure of idealization, and that the Organization may be engaging in a related psychological defense mechanism, termed "splitting"—the suppression of unacceptable positive or negative qualities of self or others.[17]

Representing a failure to combine positive and negative qualities into a whole, splitting may be particularly germane to the process of clarifying the future role of the Organization, which would benefit from taking full account of both the positive and negative aspects of its own and others' actions, present and past. This might include, for example, examining how its attitudes toward and relations with other parts of the System in which it operates—long a point of contention—contribute to productive or adverse outcomes. Likewise, the Organization could comprehensively review its conduct during times of crisis. An honest appraisal of both matters could lead it to a deeper, more complete understanding of its existing and possible future identity.

Chosen Glory: The Idealization of Crises

Dealing with crises, as suggested by many Respondents, represents the epitome of the Organization's purpose and role. Particularly in the nostalgia streams, dealing with crises is seen as demonstrating its power and external impact. As noted previously, crises also seem to bring special unity to the Organization, providing moving examples of employee dedication and personal sacrifice. As one Respondent said, "In sacrificing, we're going to contribute to the public good." Having participated in five such crises over the last 30 years, I am absolutely convinced that they are examples of outstanding institutional and individual heroism.

However, such crises can generate a particular mode of idealization within organizations called "chosen glory." This refers to a shared mental and emotional representation of an event perceived as a triumph over adversaries or a calamity, which is repeatedly cited to bolster a group's self-esteem, becoming part of an organization's identity, and passed onto succeeding generations of employees.[18] The power of chosen glory in the Organization is strongly present throughout the Conversations. This is probably inevitable, because, in fundamental ways, it exists to respond to periods of external distress and urgency. Still, as with the unquestioned rectitude of its purpose, there appears to be little interest within the Organization in considering the entirety of its actions with respect to past crises—for instance, how it might have, in fact, contributed not only to their "glorious" resolutions but also to their creation.

Fault Lines: The Idealization of Leadership and Community

Both nostalgic and postalgic streams express a longing for inspirational leadership. Such leadership seems to have two main features, vision and personal connectedness. As described by Respondents, vision provides an energizing, expansive, concrete direction for the work of the Organization. And connectedness means personal engagement and commitment from leaders toward employees, extending, at most, to a "care" for colleagues that is reminiscent of a close family. The most surprising single finding in the study, for me, was the identification of the Chief from 25 years ago as a kind of ideal inspirational leader, with hardly a mention of any prior or subsequent Chiefs. As one Ghost put it, the Chief embodied "what we believed." As nostalgia, this memory must have included aspects of idealization—though perhaps not excessively, as every Respondent who cited the Chief's leadership qualities also mentioned his all-too-human flaws.

As demonstrated by this Chief, the character of its leadership is the most important factor in determining the kind of caring community that exists in the Organization. However, a divergence appears in the definition of what that "care" should entail. Some Respondents continue to nurture nostalgia for the "family" of the past. Others in the Organization call instead for greater "togetherness." As revealed in the postalgic streams, there is a desire for increased group "unity," along with greater acceptance of individuals and acknowledgment of the value of their work. In addition, many Respondents decried the persistent divisions among employees who are considered "in" and those who are viewed as "out." Such "fault lines" can lead to conflict, impaired processes, and decreased performance.[19,20] Most prominently, Respondents reported that it can take 5 to 7 years before a new employee is truly considered to be part of the Organization, for example, before their views receive more than polite "airtime" and are taken seriously. As one Respondent explained, "You have to earn your space, and even when you do, it's brief." Many Respondents also indicated that there is a continuing, though lessening, distinction made between those who experienced the "chosen glory" of the 2008 crisis, and those who did not. Another longstanding fault line, reviewed earlier, runs between official and nonofficial level employees in the Organization, as exemplified by the promotion and holiday party matters.

By-Products of Idealization: Resistance to Change and Lack of Psychological Safety

Idealization and its related psychodynamic forces lead to two aspects of the organization that could have a pervading impact on the fulfillment of its purpose and role, how it views crises, the nature of its leadership, and the type of community it ultimately becomes. Arising mostly in the postalgia streams, these aspects concern the resistance to change and the lack of psychological safety in the Organization.

Respondents suggested several causes for the resistance to change, including the lack of an animating crisis, a general fear of change stemming from risk aversion, discomfort with uncertainty, the threat of possible punishments, pessimism, and avoidance. As mentioned earlier, underlying many of these factors may be the idealization of the past, particularly that of the "chosen glory." Such idealization could support a collective fantasy that, because the Organization successfully dealt with previous crises, it will be able to do so again. This fantasy could bolster social defenses in the organization against change. "Social defenses" serve the purpose of reinforcing a group's defenses against fundamental anxieties in the workplace.[21] Change, by its nature, creates anxiety. To assuage this anxiety, and as supported by Junior and Staffer accounts, social defenses in the organization may be operating to provide undue confidence in existing practices, downplay future risks, and so deny the need for change.

Many Respondents also feel a disturbing lack of psychological safety in the Organization. This broadly refers to the safety to speak, to be wrong, to disagree, to surface unacknowledged conflict, and, perhaps encapsulating them all, the safety to learn. The idealization of a successful past lays the foundation for this environment of fear. Learning necessarily involves anxiety, for individuals and groups.[22] It is uncomfortable to replace what is well known and has worked in the past with something new. This inherent unease increases with the fear that the new learning may involve possible failure, asking for help, or admitting a mistake in front of others. Respondents from all Cohorts, especially those voicing postalgic desires, cited an underlying and ever-present anxiety around their freedom to speak up and learn in safety. Admitted one, "I spend a lot of time feeling afraid—it needs to be more OK to be wrong." This anxiety can be reduced by an environment that supports interpersonal risk taking, where no one will embarrass, reject, or punish someone else for expressing their opinions.[23] Respondents echoed this prescription, citing three specific shifts in attitude that are needed in the organization: an openness to seeing things anew; an assumption of good intent by all participants; and engagement with—not just tolerance of—differing views.

Theoretical Concepts Revisited

The definition of nostalgia as a warm longing for a former time when the organization was more like an extension of a caring family was clearly in evidence.[24] The study also seems to corroborate many of the positive attributes of nostalgia, such as the preservation of group self-esteem, support for uniqueness claims, and shared feelings of pride and affiliation in the Organization.[25,26] However, an important finding of my research is the role that nostalgia might play in creating and exacerbating in-group/out-group feelings within an organization, as described earlier.

For its part, postalgia is described as an activating force that is energizing, anticipatory, and hopeful, while simultaneously creating anxiety, doom, and foreboding. I found that postalgia in the Organization, when ignited, very much reflects this latter set of feelings, rather than a positive vision of rationalist, instrumental prowess. In addition, postalgic thinking—such as long-term or strategic thinking—is typically considered the natural domain of the senior managerial class.[27] However, in my research, the Juniors, not the Seniors, exhibited the most intense postalgia in the Organization. It may be that the younger generation, with their future careers ahead of them, are more prone to postalgic thinking than their elders. Whatever the reason, it appears that postalgia can be strongly felt by a wide variety of organizational members.

Creating a Transitional Zone: The Interplay of Nostalgia and Postalgia

It is notable that past research on nostalgia and postalgia has failed to consider how the two interplay, how they can coexist in an organization, and, more importantly, how they might be understood and deployed together to advance organizations in times of change. For example, are nostalgia and postalgia naturally and fundamentally "at war" with each other? Or is there a way to combine their respective golden memories and shining desires into a welcome present and future?

As a mixed, shifting emotion, nostalgia provides license for a wide range of perceptions depending on its context and can enable individuals and groups to see themselves as adaptive over time.[28] Might postalgia, as a similarly ambivalent, idealized feeling, in fact be well suited for a flexible, productive partnership with nostalgia?

Organizational transition theories provide a view into how this interplay might proceed. All-important in facilitating this process appears to be the creation of a "transitional zone" where the ramifications of possible endings and beginnings can be considered, fully felt, and processed.[29] This transitional zone involves recognition that learning is painful, and that adaptation takes time and involves both a "letting go" and a building on the past. The question in this zone is not only "Of all that we care about, what must be given up to survive and thrive going forward?" but also "What must be preserved into the future, or we will lose precious values, core competencies, and lose who we are?"[30]

Living Through the Transitional Zone:
Lessons From the Ghosts

Although none of the Respondents were specifically asked about the interplay of nostalgia and postalgia or transitions to a new identity, the Ghosts' accounts seemed to provide insights into the experience of such profound change. In varying ways, the Ghosts appear to have reconciled their nostalgic pasts, the subsequent shifts in the organization, their individual postalgic desires, and their new pursuits in life. In the Conversations, each revealed a personal awareness that seemed to underlie or transcend whatever nostalgic or postalgic feelings they carried in relation to the Organization. Their stories may provide guideposts for current employees in how to acknowledge and work with the nostalgic and postalgic narratives in the organization as it seeks to further clarify its collective identity.

Ghost 1

One Ghost recounted feeling "out of joint" with the Organization prior to deciding to leave it. He thought that the Organization had changed significantly, leading him to repeatedly wonder, "Why are *they* all acting like this?" After greater introspection and consideration, this question gradually changed to, "Is it them—or is it me?" The Ghost explained, "It's all too easy to say the Organization should always be the way it was, and they should all be like me. But that would be a very narcissistic view." Instead, he said, "I realized I'm different now, and that feeling was a signal that it was time for me to move on." Most strikingly, he was "no longer convinced that the old way is still the right way."

Ghost 2

Another Ghost described his decision to leave the Organization as particularly painful because it was so integral to his identity—"it was who I was." In addition, the Ghost's contribution to the Organization may not have been widely appreciated, and many of those who did value it have now passed away. This has led to his awareness of what was truly important during his time in the Organization, and now: relationships.

"People trusted me. Those relationships were all that mattered," he said. "The most important thing to me continues to be the integrity of my relationships. Those are real."

Ghost 3

After leaving the Organization, another Ghost reported "feeling like there was a weight lifted off my shoulders that I didn't know I was carrying around." This stemmed from "not being able to let go of the Organization's old identity." Since then, the Ghost has heard about changes in the Organization, including, most recently, the new holiday party. She was pleasantly surprised by what was reported, so much so that she feels sad not to be included in the new changes. "I want people to thrive," said the Ghost, "and I feel like I missed an important moment in the life of the Organization." Several weeks after the party, the Ghost even dreamt that she was an outsider, witnessing a positive new direction in the Organization. Afterward, the Ghost was stunned by the realization that "the things that may be good for the Organization now are completely different from what I was nostalgic for."

Ghost 4

"I worked very hard on not missing this place," said this Ghost. Over the years, the Organization had become part of his life and self—a kind of "second nature." The Ghost tries not to get "emotionally involved" with the changes in it and aims to continue to live according to its values, albeit in other settings. These include "the idea of mission, purpose, service to others, and giving back." This Ghost concluded by saying, "It's about working toward the greater good—that's where my heart lies."

These stories of these four Ghosts do not provide a comprehensive strategy for moving through a transition that involves dealing with nostalgia and postalgia. They don't set out a way to adjudicate competing claims about what should be given up and what should be conserved, nor delineate a singular path toward a final resolution. More than anything, they each describe a kind of "psychic posture" by which the Ghosts now understand and approach their lives.

None of them renounced the "rightness" of the Organization's, nor their own pasts, and each expressed a fundamental realization that sustains and impels them through changing times. For Ghost 1, this involved a thorough acceptance of changes within the organization and himself—and the possibility that the old ways might no longer be the best. Similarly, Ghost 3 experienced the surprising insight that, although different from what had been nostalgically valued, change can in fact lead to new kinds of thriving. Ghosts 2 and 4 professed their abiding devotion to certain values that had always grounded and guided their lives, both in and outside of the Organization: trusted relationships and service to others.

The Ghosts' psychic postures toward change seem highly relevant for the Organization and its future challenges. Without additional information from the Ghosts, it is impossible to know precisely how these postures came about—though, even from the little the Ghosts said, one can detect the painful learning, adaptation over time, and the "letting go" and "building upon" that are described in the transition theories. The Ghosts have remained true to their most cherished values, while also likely making use of the ambiguous, shifting aspects of both nostalgia and postalgia to understand their own identities. In effect, they seem to have each gone beyond nostalgia and postalgia to discover the feelings and values that lie deeper still. This discovery seems to have enabled them to change. Adopting the psychic postures of the Ghosts—reflecting on what truly matters and endures through past, present, and future—may prove to be a powerful way for members of the Organization to begin to approach each other and their differences as they come to understand their nostalgic memories and postalgic desires, and look to forge its new collective identity.

General Applications of Methodology and Findings

My research demonstrates the usefulness of paying close attention to nostalgia and postalgia as a method of understanding the existing state of an organization. Asking just two questions, one about nostalgia and the other about postalgia, provided a tremendous amount of data about employees' perceptions and feelings about the current state of the Organization. While these data may not yield the entire story, it suggests that taking account of nostalgia and postalgia can be a very effective tool for those concerned with diagnosing organizational culture.

Perhaps most importantly, the study highlights the central importance of the past in organizations. The study reveals—for better or worse—the great significance that the past can have within an organization in defining its collective identity and in how it functions. This strongly suggests that, rather than ignoring or denying the past, leaders need to be more aware of the continuous power of the past within their organizations. The past itself may not be subject to "control," but I believe that this study has shown the need for leaders to be far more conscious of and responsive to it.

The evocation of nostalgia and postalgia could also be helpful to leaders or practitioners as they try to assist organizations moving through transitions. Though not actually shown as such in the study, it seems plausible that raising nostalgic memories and postalgic desires could facilitate a dialogue about "what must be given up" and "what must be conserved" during times of transition in an organization's collective identity.

In the case of the Organization, the identification and analysis of the streams of nostalgia and postalgia, along with the recognition of psychodynamic forces that appear to be present, revealed the key issues the organization should address to move forward. Fundamentally, it needs to courageously explore its enduring memories and evoke its future desires. Its leaders, in particular, must be unafraid to see the entirety of its being—both positive and negative—and to understand the resistance and fear that arises when its longings and dreams are not felt or accepted. Only then will the necessary inspiration and sense of community arise to recreate its collective identity.

Upon completion of the study, I confirmed the broad validity of my methodology and findings through individual discussions with 40 of the senior leaders and employees of the Organization. I also shared the study with a number of others—for example, the head of a public relations agency, the chief administrator of a synagogue, and the managing partner of a major investment firm—none of whom had any connection with the Organization. All these readers, both within the Organization and outside, reported that they immediately related to the study and that it set off their own organizational memories and desires; enabled them to understand others' feelings and reflect on their own behaviors; and powerfully framed challenges related to collective identity in new and actionable ways.

To elicit similar results from studies on the influence of nostalgia and postalgia in other organizations, I recommend the following general guidelines:

- Interview a broad cross-section of employees and leaders in the organization. Seniors, Juniors, Staffers, and Ghosts all contributed different perspectives to the study.
- Ask a small number of open-ended questions—two is ideal— to avoid directing respondents toward certain immediate responses and encourage deep reflection.
- Once you have collected the open, wide-ranging responses to your questions, look for the major nostalgic or postalgic themes or "streams" that unite different responses.
- Seek out the psychodynamic forces that lie beneath the surface of the streams.
- Finally, look for the emotional currents that bring the streams together.

Final Thoughts

For me, researching and writing this study has been a true "journey from nearness to distance—and back."[31] I was well aware of the essential and profound dedication of the Organization and its people to serving others, especially in times of crisis. But seeing the organization from the new and further vantage points of the nostalgic and postalgic streams, and with the aid of psychodynamic lenses, has given me a much more complete and intimate picture of the emotional context in which this dedication to service exists, and the dilemmas it faces.

It could seem, to some readers, that I have overemphasized a collection of very harmful out-of-consciousness factors in the Organization, such as holding an idealized image of itself, hanging on to outdated tales of glory, engaging in social defenses against change, and propagating an environment which spawns anxiety and fear. But, at the same time, the organization maintains strong ideals, its past triumphs inspire and sustain its ongoing work and group cohesion, its steadfastness underpins its indispensable stability, and its deliberative practices ensure careful, thoughtful decision making.

Seeing, for the first time, the complexity of the Organization's emotional drivers has given me a fresh appreciation of the fundamental need of its employees: to connect with others through a shared purpose. Throughout this study, by virtue of the acknowledgment and expression of their good and true memories and heartfelt desires, nothing radiated more warmly or ran more deeply and constantly than their longing for community and togetherness in fulfilling a vitally important public mission.

CHAPTER 4

Raising Awareness and Recovering Agency in the Face of Narcissistic Leadership

Fernanda Pomin

Introduction

Approximately 1 percent of the population falls within the psychopath category, and around 3.9 percent of corporate professionals can be described as having psychopathic tendencies.[1] Among the various existing pathologies in the corporate world, pathological narcissism is the dysfunction most frequently found at senior levels.[2]

There is a tendency within organizations to seek out people for leadership positions who exhibit many of the characteristics of narcissists, assuming such roles require those traits.[3,4] Consequently, narcissistic people end up reaching higher organizational positions due to their charismatic and manipulative personality, and despite their excessive drive and ambition.[5] This gives many people working in organizations a fair chance of experiencing a toxic working environment.

Navigating the complex waters of narcissistic leadership is therefore one of the most typical challenges faced by people working in organizations. Staying humble as you step up the corporate ladder is a tough challenge. It takes such self-confidence and competence to reach the top of an organization that it might be difficult not to get drunk on your own success when you get there. But do these leaders become less humble when they get there, or do they get there *because* they are overly self-confident?

The topic of toxic leadership and the complexity of the corporate environment have always been appealing to me. Having worked as a specialist in Leadership Development and Culture Change for global companies and consultancies for 27 years, I often witnessed these dynamics firsthand. The phenomena that fascinated me the most were those related to the relationship between leaders and followers.

I remember, many years ago, being especially intrigued by a popular saying in the corporate world: "People leave their leaders, not their organizations." This observation has stayed with me since the beginning of my career and motivated me to seek answers and explanations for these complex corporate dynamics.

Was Steve Jobs a narcissist? Is Donald Trump? What about Jair Bolsonaro?

Labeling these people as clinically narcissistic is difficult, perhaps even impossible, and was not the intent of my research. Rather, my entry point was to look instead at the subordinates themselves, placing importance on their voices, perceptions, and experiences. But this is a double-edged sword: When narcissism goes unchecked, it has the potential to become damaging to an organization and kill the morale of those working under such leaders.

I was fortunate to have had wonderful leaders who taught me immensely. But there were also the ones who made me reflect about the destructive potential that leaders can have on teams' morale and motivation, taking my interest in the dark side of the leadership to a higher level.

I once received a global "Client Excellence Award" from the organization I was working for. Only one person worldwide was elected in the business unit for which I responded. I was extremely happy and proud of myself and my team, pleased to have so much effort recognized. After the official recognition rituals, my boss called me into his office and told me that I also had something to worry about. Finally, he told me that meeting my clients' expectations should not be my number one priority, since my focus should be on the origination of new deals, above anything else.

That was a nice bucket of cold water! With not much more than half a dozen words, my boss was able to take me from heaven to hell! From all that euphoria and feeling of accomplishment, there was only a bitter taste left in the end. As hard as I tried, I could not help but brood inside myself if that award were an acknowledgment for something I had done very right, or perhaps very wrong.

Please raise your hand if you have never had a difficult leader!

Breaking open the gridlock found in organizations plagued by leadership that is infused with narcissistic tendencies was the central focus of my research. What you will find in this chapter is a summary of the key findings of a study conducted on successful and unsuccessful subordinates' experiences when dealing with leaders perceived as narcissistic. My main purpose was to better understand what it takes for subordinates to deal with these leaders in such a way that allows them to perform successfully, instead of feeling demoralized, devalued, and victimized.

Since narcissistic leaders will probably not change, the idea is to consider alternative strategies that allow their subordinates not only to survive but also *(why not?)* to immunize themselves against narcissism. By engaging directly with those who mostly suffer the side effects of such leadership and moving away from blaming the narcissistic leader, I present a more pragmatic approach to protect one's mental health and working capacity under such leadership.

Now, besides thinking about the narcissistic leaders you may have crossed with in your journey, I also invite you to put yourself in their shoes and consider whether some of the insights you will find in this chapter may also apply to you.

Methodology

The central part of my study derived from a thematic analysis of a series of interviews with direct reports of C-suite leaders perceived by them as narcissistic. All of my interviewees came from large national and multinational corporations, where narcissistic leaders seem to flourish and where there are political games in place, as well as fights for power and influence. Fifty percent of the executives interviewed reported directly into a CEO and 50 percent reported to a C-suite leader; 33 percent were male and 67 percent were female; and the age range varied between 40 and 68.

There was also a good distribution among different industry segments and working functions, all within the Brazilian cultural environment.

Since most people tend to get emotional when talking about notably negative experiences with toxic leaders, it was key to make use of some socioanalytic methods[6]—such as "free associating" and "discovering critical incidents." In order to "jolt" the imagination of the interviewees, I started the conversation with a pack of cards that have a specially selected set of photographs, illustrations, and words, and I asked people to choose the cards that would best describe their past experience working with those leaders. Following this "Free-Association" phase, qualitative research in the form of semistructured interviews was provided for the empirical base of the study. By tapping into their unconscious, and thus taking a different path for assessing knowledge and experience, I was able to start from an experiential point of view, rather than a theoretical one. These in-depth interviews were then analyzed for common themes and repeating patterns, and possible approaches which might facilitate or hinder the success of those relationships were identified.

The Dark Side of Leadership

In times of crisis and change, when the level of complexity and uncertainty is high, executives are confronted with the need to manage increasing levels of pressure and stress. In order to cope with that stress, defense mechanisms typically arise, leading many leaders to reveal their darker side.

Although most people occupying leadership positions do not present significant mental problems, a surprising number of senior executives do have a personality disorder of some kind.[2] While sound and stable leaders allow employees to focus on performing their jobs well, leaders who are not willing to deal with the shadow side of power might generate corporate dynamics capable of destroying people and organizations.[7,8,9]

Tough or demanding leaders do not necessarily fall into the pathological category as long as they are respectful and fair, and their primary goal is to obtain the best performance from their people.[10] Often, however, it can be difficult to differentiate what is pathological from what is only difficult, demanding, and tiring. Especially when we are subjected to such situations, or when we feel pressured or unfairly treated.

Kets de Vries helps us understand what pathological manifestations of leadership are. According to him, there are two types of psychopaths: the "heavy" and the "light" ones. Heavy psychopaths are born "without the ability to form emotional bonds" due to possible genetic abnormalities.[11] They are often immortalized in the history of mankind, such as Adolf Hitler, Josef Stalin, Saddam Hussein, or Bachar al-Assad from Syria. Other times, they are portrayed in fictional characters, such as the unforgettable Hannibal Lecter, from *The Silence of the Lambs*.

Many of the lighter type become successful executives, proliferating in environments where power, control, status, or money is at stake. To our misfortune, however, toxic executives with light psychopathic tendencies are more difficult to identify, as they can easily adapt to certain organizational environments. Despite their incapacity to experience "normal" feelings like shame, guilt, or remorse, many of these executives will go unnoticed because of their ability to manipulate, both downward with their subordinates and upward with their superiors.[12] Obviously, they would not survive if they did not have some of the most valued skills in the corporate world. It is difficult to imagine a highly toxic and deeply incompetent executive being protected by his superiors. On the other hand, it is not at all difficult to imagine highly seductive people, extremely intelligent and endowed with specific and scarce talents, being acclaimed by those who benefit from their contribution. As they are intelligent, they are also able to discern where and when they should behave in a certain way. That is exactly why organizations begin to not only tolerate but also unconsciously encourage this type of dysfunctional behavior.

The Pathological Narcissist

Narcissism is not something that a person has or does not have, since we all have narcissistic characteristics to a certain degree. Possessing a healthy dose of narcissism works as a defense mechanism and is necessary to survive, since "assertiveness, self-confidence, tenacity, and creativity just can't exist without it"[13]—*at last, something that not only explains but also justifies the fact that we are all narcissists, to some degree!* However, many senior executives fail because they become too full of themselves. "Caught in the web of narcissism, they lose their ability to consider alternative ways of doing things."[14]

Jung introduced the concept of shadow in 1917 as "the negative side of the personality, the sum of all those unpleasant qualities we like to hide, together with the insufficiently developed functions and the content of the personal unconscious."[15] According to Jung, our key life purpose is to discover and integrate all parts of the self. Since leadership roles have also a shadow side, many leaders are tempted to equate themselves with their roles, falling into the trap of feeling above the rules, special and more important than others, thus losing perspective.[16] Leaders need to realize that their leadership success and legacy depend on learning from and integrating their shadows. By facing their own vulnerabilities and expanding their level of consciousness about themselves, they can strengthen and expand their capabilities and positive impact.[17] On the other hand, failing to integrate their shadows hinders self-awareness, allowing dysfunctional leadership behaviors, such as narcissism, not only to emerge but also to fester.

The greatest antidote against the dark side of leadership is, therefore, enhancing leadership self-awareness. *But how realistic is it to expect this to happen voluntarily?*

Narcissism Defined

The Greek myth of Narcissus tells the story of a beautiful young man who fell in love with his own reflection while gazing into a pool of water. Captured by the sight of his beauty, Narcissus kept admiring his reflection and died in despair when realizing that he would be unable to seduce his own image.[18]

Narcissism is one of the most confusing concepts in psychoanalysis, being that the available empirical literature is both complex and vague. The lack of consensus about the narcissistic personality encompasses "everything from a self-oriented motivational state, a normal phase of psychological development, a configuration of personality traits, to a personality disorder."[19]

These different views on narcissism result, among other things, from the individual experience people have with narcissistic personalities. But the narcissistic personality manifests itself in different degrees, from what can be considered a "natural" level of narcissism (presented by many of us) to what we could call pathological, when narcissism becomes harmful or even toxic.

While the discussion of narcissism has recently become very popular, the psychological study of narcissism dates back to more than one century ago. Freud first wrote about the differences between "primary, but not clinical narcissism, as the extent to which individuals are driven by self-love, and secondary narcissism as a form of personality disorder."[20]

In organizational psychology, narcissism is defined as a personality trait entailing a grandiose sense of the self (paired with self-affirmative strategies and disregard for others), existing in all individuals, albeit to varying degrees, rather than a mental illness.[21]

Before moving on, let's look at a story that might help us understand how narcissists behave:

Once upon a time, I was invited to present a coaching proposal to a CEO. In our first meeting, I asked him what he would like to develop that would justify his search for coaching. He told me that he didn't really know what he needed to develop. In that case, I suggested an assessment process in the first place, so that we could together decide whether coaching was really necessary. I conducted the assessment process based on individual interviews with himself and his direct reports. As I believed that his interest in his own development was genuine, I made my best effort to offer him something of value as a result of the evaluation process. I thought to myself: I need to be able to point out his strengths as a CEO, but also any relevant aspects that will allow him to leverage his performance in the future. Convinced that I had done a good job, I scheduled the feedback session. Everything was going well while I was addressing his strengths. When I started mentioning his developmental opportunities, however, he got visibly irritated and started to question everything. One of the points I raised was about his political ability. He had told me that he usually got deeply impatient when interacting with other CEOs, as well as when taking external courses, claiming that executives within his market segment were not as intellectually advanced as he was, and that the previous courses he had taken had no added value. He also did not mind express-

ing his frustration, positioning himself in an extremely critical and arrogant manner. I challenged him to consider whether his posture might generate less appetite for possible partnerships, mergers, acquisitions, or even information sharing. Getting more and more irritated, he exclaimed: "Steve Jobs was also not politically skilled, and that did not harm his career!" I finally realized that I was facing an executive who not only compared himself to Steve Jobs, but who also ignored opportunities for self-improvement. This example allowed me to understand what happens when self-confidence crosses the line and turns into arrogance.

Driven by grandiose fantasies about themselves, pathological narcissists are selfish and inconsiderate, demand excessive attention, feel entitled, and pursue power and prestige at all costs. They live in a binary world where people are either "for" or "against" them, and enjoy believing that they are totally in control.[22,23]

Narcissistic individuals can become very impatient or get quite angry when they don't receive the special treatment that they believe they deserve due to their strong sense of entitlement. It is also difficult for them to recognize or identify with the feelings and needs of others (low empathy), and they have a hard time handling criticism, feeling easily hurt, overreacting, and getting defensive.[24]

In short: it is a lot safer not to provoke their anger!

A lot has also been said about the "paradox of narcissism," which lies within this disregard for others, while also seeking for their approval. Although pathological narcissists may seem very confident and often give off an impression of having high self-esteem, that confidence masks deep vulnerability as they are troubled by a strong sense of insecurity.[25] Since they are trying to compensate for narcissistic wounds ("blows to their self-esteem that were inflicted in childhood by parents who were either too distant or too indulgent"[26]), people with narcissistic injuries are always in search of an admiring audience that can feed their hunger for recognition and external affirmation.[27]

Although narcissists may not intend to harm others, they fail to maintain positive social relationships in the long run due to their recurring attempt to fulfill their own needs for self-affirmation and external validation, sometimes at the expense of others' well-being. In other words, narcissistic leaders appear to act from their own needs, which does not necessarily include the destruction of others, but rather their own satisfaction. As the satisfaction of their needs implies, most of the time, the decrease of those with whom they interact, this decrease is more the result of this search, than its main goal.[28]

This reminds me of the scorpion and the frog tale, which I summarize in the following section:

> *The Scorpion and The Frog is a tale about a scorpion that asks a frog to take him across a river. The frog is reluctant to help him make the crossing, as he is afraid of being bitten during the trip. The scorpion argues that if it stings the frog, it would sink and they would both drown. The frog agrees and begins to carry the scorpion, but, in the middle of the crossing, the scorpion ends up stinging the frog, condemning both to death. The frog, just before drowning, asks the scorpion why he did it. The scorpion then replies; "It is my nature. I couldn't help it."*

This metaphor makes me think of the narcissists' nature. In order to meet their own psychic needs, they end up hurting those around them. I don't mean that they should not be held responsible for the damage they cause. Quite the contrary! But perhaps, all we can do is to try to understand why they do what they do.

In order to allow a more pragmatic and experience-based description of narcissistic leadership, I proposed a new framework encompassing its most characteristic behaviors in Table 4.1.

Table 4.1 Proposed framework for narcissistic leadership

Entitlement and arrogance: Displaying disregard for others, seeing oneself as special and unique, and believing you deserve special treatment	Power and recognition: Strong need to exert influence over others, to be in control and to pursue prestige and recognition	Emotional balance and awareness: Difficulty recognizing and accepting own vulnerabilities and shortcomings, or managing own emotions

Pros and Cons of Narcissism

But is narcissistic leadership always negative?

"Many global organizations have become highly attractive to people who are eager to advance themselves at the expense of others and the companies they work for"[29] even though their dysfunctional behavior can seriously affect corporate morale and performance.

If narcissism were only harmful, why would it have proliferated so easily across the corporate world? I found out, both in literature and in my research, that there are also positive aspects arising from leadership narcissism. If it weren't for this, perhaps this "evil" would have been eradicated a long time ago.

The question of whether narcissism is good or bad is another area of great debate in existing literature. While narcissistic leaders may fail to establish positive relationships with their followers, the market not only values but also allows itself to be carried away by the ability that many narcissistic leaders have to design convincing strategies for the business. Market professionals, in general, yearn for well-articulated and ambitious proposals that allow them to believe that the future will be better than the present. Narcissistic leaders, therefore, fill this gap when they present their visionary ideas that portray a promising future.[30]

Findings also suggest, for example, that followers prefer narcissistic leaders when they feel uncertain. When individuals face situations of uncertainty and unpredictability, narcissistic leaders who exude strength, overconfidence, and toughness were preferred to other more "appropriate" leadership styles.[31] Choosing a narcissistic leader was therefore described as a coping strategy to reduce the stress and anxiety brought up by contexts of uncertainty. In times of crisis and change, what we want most is to know that everything will be fine in the end.

In this sense, narcissistic leadership seems to attend to one of our greatest expectations as human beings: feeling safe!

It seems impossible not to think about the uncertainty we have been facing during these pandemic years. Dealing with something we have never dealt with before, feeling insecure about our own health and that of our family members and colleagues, facing the reality of death day after day ...

In times like this, of enormous uncertainty, suffering, and insecurity, leaders who are sure of themselves, able to tell the population what to do or not to do, are in general more appreciated than those who are insecure or lost. Not to mention the distress generated when different leaders within the same country send dissonant messages about what should or should not be done: to wear or not the mask, social distancing or lockdown, vertical or horizontal isolation. Right or wrong, what the population expects is to be given clear directions, even if the leader needs to apologize afterward, when circumstances or new data prove them wrong.

By the way, being able to apologize for wrong decisions made in the past is something that cannot be expected from narcissistic leaders, who are likely to continue defending their theses until their last breaths, even after those had being shattered by empirical or even scientific evidence. *Looking at the pandemic in retrospect, which global leaders seem to have excelled in the narcissism ranking, in your opinion?*

Even though narcissists actively pursue leadership positions and are likely to be selected for them, their actions and decisions will not always prove effective over time, given that their main objective is to "look good in the picture," even if this generates considerable liability for the company in the future[32]—*obviously when they have long left the company!* It is worth mentioning that, more and more, the CEO's personal reputation is merging with that of the company, increasing the reputational risk on the part of companies led by executives who exhibit significant dysfunctional behaviors.

Well, so far, we have seen at least five reasons that justify the proliferation of narcissistic leaders in organizations:

1. Ability to articulate a promising vision for the future
2. Reducing stress and anxiety in times of uncertainty
3. Ensuring short-term results
4. Ability to take the necessary risks to get the job done
5. Ability to influence and persuade

All of these reasons help explain the "functionality" of narcissism in organizational systems. They are all useful skills and competences for facing different strategic challenges, especially in critical or adverse situations.

Since CEOs have been rewarded for taking risks and showing self-confidence throughout their careers, such confidence and conviction, when taken to extremes, might translate into narcissism, which can kill companies and CEO careers.[33] In this sense, narcissism can be understood as a manifestation of excessive self-confidence, being a good example of what happens when something good becomes negative. As people say: what differentiates medicine from poison is its dose!

Chamorro-Premuzic presents us with an interesting reflection to help us deepen our reflection even further:

> "Perhaps it is true that our unconscious views of leadership are rooted in archaic prehistorical archetypes, which would explain the almost universal preference for strong (and despotic) masculine risk takers over and above vulnerable, self-critical, and feminine leaders."[34]

This forces us to think about the leadership choices we make in our organizations. Narcissistic traits are not as discrete as to prevent us from recognizing them in daily life. Often, we let ourselves be seduced by these leaders, closing our eyes to the characteristics of their personalities that will haunt us in the future. Generally, such traits become even more prominent the more we empower them.

Why on earth, then, do we pretend not to notice such traits when choosing these leaders?

The purpose of my research, though, was to shed new light on how much of what was happening was consciously available to the subordinates of those leaders, so that they could do something about it. Let us look, then, from another perspective.

Are there also advantages for those working with such leaders?

To answer this question, I asked my interviewees to describe the experience of working with a narcissistic leader. Several different kinds of impact were identified, which were clustered in 11 different categories:

1. Emotional distress
2. Physical distress
3. Lack of work–life balance

4. Low self-esteem
5. Low engagement
6. Guilt
7. Exhaustion
8. Defensiveness
9. Giving up
10. Generation of new insights
11. Nostalgia

From the afore-listed 11 impacts, 9 are clearly negative. To varying degrees, all of these impacts have affected the subordinates' physical or psychological well-being. Surprisingly, two positive impacts were identified: generation of new insights and nostalgia. Both points seemed quite surprising.

- The first one refers to how much a negative, unpleasant, stressful, or simply uncomfortable experience can lead a person to reflect about their own condition. These people claimed to have been led to look at their individual situations, asking themselves why they were subjected to them, looking for explanations or even possible ways out.
- The latter concerns the pride that emerged from having worked with strong, charismatic leaders, capable of doing great things. Despite being very demanding, or perhaps because of that, these people claim to have grown under their leadership. For some people, being strongly demanded, albeit not properly, made them grow and discover new possibilities about themselves.

In view of the above, my research data seemed to confirm that narcissistic leadership indeed has both positive and negative impacts on people and organizations, depending on how you look at it.

Narcissism Perceived

"A good way to spot a narcissist is to look at how his subordinates respond to him."[35] Described as having a Dr. Jekyll and Mr. Hyde personality, narcissists can most often be seen for who they are only by the people who are "victims of their machinations."[36]

This is why I chose not to rely on their self-assessment when trying to describe their behaviors, but rather sought to understand how narcissism manifests itself in organizations, from the perspective of their main victims—their subordinates.

Maybe it is also worth taking the chance, while reading this section, to revisit your own behavior, wondering how you are perceived by the ones who interact with you.

I found a surprising level of openness and willingness when approaching people who interacted with leaders perceived as narcissistic, which raised an initial hypothesis about how much these experiences have been impactful in their professional lives, and still represented a major need for further reflection, learning, and "sense making."

By using the "free-association" method, I was able to categorize my interviewees' words, adjectives, expressions, and brief examples of how their leaders behave into seven different themes in Table 4.2.

Table 4.2 Free associations

	Clusters	Free associations
i.	Obstruction	Oppression; tyranny; hate; disrespect; manipulation; obstacles; difficulties; anguish; chaos; conflict; traffic jam; no way out
ii.	Seduction	Focus on image or appearance; superficial; too many rituals; talking to everyone; fun, charismatic
iii.	Grandiose	Demanding and tough relationships; highly persistent leaders who would not negotiate their goals; competitive people who want to be the number one all the time; ambitious; need for achievement; need to be in power, at the top, always striving for something bigger
iv.	Vanity	Needs to be on stage; wants to be the focus of everyone's attention; need for recognition; wants to show his power and be in control; may become a beast when confronted; king of the jungle
v.	Lack of authenticity	Fake; mask; caricature; not knowing what he/she thinks/feels
vi.	Trust	Lack of trust; does not trust anyone; expects blind loyalty; loyal to whomever is loyal to him; symbiotic relationship
vii.	Instability	Humor oscillation, you never know when it is a good time to approach him; humor oscillates during the day

As you can see, there is a predominantly negative emotional charge that emerges when people think about their past experiences with leaders who seem narcissistic to them. Although some associations could be considered positive (fun and charismatic), the vast majority seemed to invoke clearly undesirable experiences.

A first finding of the investigation process was the realization that most people tend to have an accurate perception of narcissistic leadership, despite their low level of expertise in this field. There were two ways to check the accuracy of their perceptions. On the one hand, I tried to understand how they would describe these leaders, deliberately remaining neutral to allow both positive and negative aspects to emerge. On the other hand, I also sought to reconfirm their perceptions by asking for concrete examples.

I highlight below some of the most illustrative critical incidents mentioned during the interviews. In total, 86 critical incidents were analyzed. Some of the stories that best represent each dimension of my proposed framework are described below.

Table 4.3 Entitlement and arrogance

He told me to change a homosexual team member to another place because he didn't want to have to look at him all day.
People from all over the country were already booked and had their flight tickets bought for the training program. She wanted to cancel it last minute to suit her personal agenda.
I asked him for a salary raise and he said: "Doesn't your husband have a good salary?"
I reached out to him for support in a complex situation involving one of our key clients. He said: "I am confident that you have all the skills to find the solution to this problem by yourself, but if, after giving it a second try you still cannot make it, please come back to me and I will be happy to assist you."
I spent the whole weekend preparing a manual he had asked me for. When I presented it to him, he threw it on the floor saying that it was a "piece of shit." I cried in the bathroom afterward.

The examples shown in Table 4.3 indicate a strong contempt for the other and reveal a belief in their own superiority and importance, allowing them to feel entitled to be treated in a special and differentiated way. Their attitudes seem to derive from the thought, belief, or conviction that "the world spins around them!"

Table 4.4 Power and recognition

When she took over as my boss, she told me: "You will no longer talk to the CEO, since I will do that, but you can count on my full support for whatever you need."
When challenged by one of his direct reports who had contacted one of his peers directly to check the information provided by him, he fired that person claiming he no longer fit with the organization.
She told her team that they would be in trouble if she ever found out about any decisions taken without her awareness or if she was ever in a meeting where there was a discussion about anything that she should have been previously informed of and was not.
The organization was implementing the Casual Friday policy, which he was completely against. After never-ending discussions, he finally agreed, but only if all employees from his area would be wearing the company's t-shirt (he created his own special policy).
When I told him that I was upset about the person who was going to be fired and replaced by me, he told me: "You only owe loyalty to me, nobody else!"

In these examples, the behavior of the leader reveals an expressive concern with power and territory. They need to have control, to strongly influence the behavior of others, and to have prestige. Here, the belief behind their actions seems to follow a popular Brazilian saying that states something like: "the ones in a position of power, tell others what to do; the wise ones obey".

Table 4.5 Emotional balance and awareness

After a few people resigned from her team, she called me to say how well we got along. I replied: "Yes, we surely do, but you know it is also very complex." She agreed and ended the conversation.
He approved the new commercial policy without some of its basic assumptions. As the results started not to come in, I insisted several times on its revision. It took him more than a year to agree to adjust it, but he blamed the Financial Director and never admitted his responsibility.
When she got a bad performance review, she told me it was due to her team, which "sucked."
She did not want me to talk to the CEO directly, but when we had a problem with an external provider, which would have a strong impact in one of our key projects, she told me to go talk to him and explain the situation myself.
I gave her honest feedback three times. She told me I had to understand she was German, and that was how German people behaved.

These last examples suggest enormous difficulty in recognizing their responsibility when things do not go according to plan, besides an undisguised inability to hear what they don't want to hear. In this case, we can say that their motto could be something like: "I won, we are even, and you lost!"

Not only did I find out that real-life experiences by nonexperts in Organizational Psychology do match up with theories about leadership narcissism, but I also had the opportunity to validate my proposed framework for defining leadership narcissism. Even though most people may not be literate in theories regarding leadership narcissism and be ready to define what it is, they do recognize a narcissistic leader when they face one.

Additional evidence of the accurate perception of subordinates came in a couple of comments made about some of their leaders, such as "he is not evil or bad intentioned," while others used words like "manipulative, abusive, and machiavellic." We could argue that subordinates do have a good sense of whether they are dealing with a tough leader, a narcissistic one, or a darker one, such as a sociopath. It seems that common sense once again prevails when people deepen their reflection on the negative experiences they have had with their leaders.

Anyway, we should avoid labeling executives, be it in an appreciative or pejorative way. First, because no one is the owner of the truth. Second, because labeling people do not add anything to their development, much less to ours!

Coping Strategies

Having experienced narcissistic leadership may lead you to fall into the "victim syndrome." While there is truth in what you experience in a toxic working environment, believing you have no control over undesirable situations may give you a pleasant feeling of innocence, but also an uncomfortable sense of impotence.

However, dealing with leadership narcissism is especially challenging if the pathological leadership behavior is coming from the very top of the organization. Such pathological behaviors will create an atmosphere of fear and intimidation that prevent people from speaking up.[1] Instead of directing their energy toward organizational goals, employees try to remain silent to avoid further damage, putting informed decision making at risk.[37]

The famous expression "kill the messenger" was not created by chance. Saying what cannot be said, providing unsolicited feedback, or raising issues that have been swept under the rug has cost thousands of jobs out there. What about the possible consequences of telling narcissistic leaders that they are not perfect?

One aspect that drew my attention was the fact that only 17 percent of the people interviewed have sought help, either through coaching or therapy. Reaching out for help as soon as you realize something (very) wrong is going on in your relationship with your leader confirms your ability to step back and look from the balcony while walking through your personal and professional hardships.

In much fewer cases, though, there was conscious recognition that their behavior reinforced the leader's behavior, or that there was some personal gain in remaining in the toxic relationship. In other words, most people are not aware of their role in these relationships, being able to see the responsibility of the leader only, but not their own.

At last, people who seemed "stronger," moving forward with courage and resilience, may have done it without fully realizing (consciously) the existing emotional damage. The hypothesis that I raise in this case is that excessively resilient people may persist in a toxic relationship more as a defense mechanism, than through a conscious choice. Not giving up may indicate a less reflective *modus operandi*. In this case, their behavior serves as a protective shield so that they do not have to face their own vulnerability.

Now, if you are in a toxic relationship and know that narcissistic leaders are less willing to change, what can you do about it?

Since changing pathological leadership behavior is a highly complex process and rarely effective, the best strategy for subordinates might well be to develop coping mechanisms for survival and self-protection.

Confronting narcissists with the truth is dangerous and risky. If you want to establish a relationship with them, you should first convey empathy and respect, and acknowledge his or her need to be recognized.[38] In other words, to establish a connection, you must be willing to offer them what they need the most: attention and recognition!

The first thing to do when dealing with narcissistic leaders is to recognize that what is going on is a reflection of their own insecurities, shortcomings, failings, and incompetence. Second, you need to accept that some of these leaders possess a kind of mindset that is extremely hard to change. Third, you should ask yourself if you are prepared to report transgressions, or if you rather become a "silent bystander," choosing silence instead of confrontation. You should also keep in mind that they are formidable adversaries, in particular when they occupy a senior position in the company. If they are the CEO, the best option might be to move on to a healthier organization.

But which coping strategies were proven more effective?

All of the strategies below derived from "learning-from-experience" situations described by the interviewees, whether they proved successful or not. Observing what seemed to work best and worst with those leaders urged these people to adapt their own behaviors in the hope of developing a survival strategy.

I was able to identify several coping strategies that seemed to serve different purposes. They are clustered below for further clarity.

Table 4.6 Influence strategies

Approach the leaders in private when trying to persuade them, never in public
Bring other people they respect along to support you
Feed their "ego" in a clever way, pay respect to their "throne," and tell them what they want to hear
Learn to choose the right moment due to usual humor oscillation
Highlight "what's in it for them," mainly in relation to reputation, status, or results (feed their vanity)

Table 4.7 Relationship-building strategies

Bring them closer to you and invite them to get to know your business better
Find their "Achilles' heel" and discover their vulnerability to be able to offer them something of value

Influence and *relationship-building strategies* suggest proactive actions to cause the leader to approach you, accepting your suggestions and better understanding your points, allowing for some support. These are more optimistic strategies, used by people who still believe that something can be done. Essentially, what these people are looking for is to build a relationship of trust with the leader, so that they are seen as allies, instead of potential enemies.

Table 4.8 Self-protection strategies

Adapt to their style, be submissive, be their "right arm," and ask for their blessing
Protect your boss from negative exposure, warn them about any risks, and make them look better
Never challenge, confront, or disagree (specially directly), and do not be naive, assertive, or frank
Never bypass them or invade their territory, and make sure they are well informed
Focus on your performance and deliver on your goals so that they do not have a reason to chase you

Table 4.9 Avoidance strategies ("flight")

Put all your energy on your team and clients, and deviate your attention from your leader
Get help through coaching or therapy, and try to understand what belongs to you and/or to them
Avoid them, withdraw, and do not ask for help in complex or risky situations
Get yourself another job or just leave

Those of *self-protection* and *avoidance ("flight")* are both reactive, probably used by people who do not feel strong enough to confront the narcissistic leader. The safest alternative to them is the one that makes them "invisible." In such cases, the person avoids getting into the narcissistic leader's "firing line" by either taking a totally submissive position or focusing on other priorities, or even by leaving the company.

Table 4.10 Ground-standing strategies ("fight")

Stand your ground firmly and courageously, and never believe they "own your soul"
Make sure you have enough savings to allow you to make your choices freely
Confront them in an extreme and aggressive way, and be courageous

The *ground-standing* strategy *("fight")* is an extreme and quite risky alternative. Whoever chooses this strategy is either very brave or desperate! These people risk everything by confronting the narcissistic leader. They may not care about possible consequences or may not have much to lose. In this sense, the risk of losing their job can be a calculated risk, which gives them the courage for such a bold move. Curiously, it does work sometimes!

In conclusion, several strategies can be suggested so that subordinates can better manage these toxic relationships. What will be highlighted below, though, is what I consider to be the main common principles behind most successful strategies:

1. Look from the balcony! Get external support from a therapist or a coach, if necessary, and do it as soon as you realize there is something wrong going on.
2. Learn to accept your own vulnerability. Not knowing how to manage such difficult relationships is no reason to be ashamed. Admitting your struggles requires courage and self-confidence.
3. Never let a narcissistic leader "own your soul." Make sure you have what it takes to protect your freedom of choice (including financial savings). Not being fearful makes you stronger, allowing you more "space to maneuver."
4. Know thyself! Do not ever postpone thinking about other "possible selves" and finding out what gives meaning to your life. It will be helpful to guide your hardest choices and decisions in both life and work.
5. Take the driver's seat. Do not wait until things get solved by themselves or the damage may be immeasurable. Choosing to stay and choosing to leave are both acts of will, as well as choosing to be fired. But be sure to be the one who is choosing!

One last comment before moving on: these different approaches seem also applicable in contexts of high complexity, such as change, crisis, and uncertainty. Possibly, our preferred way of facing change and unexpected situations may well follow one of the five strategies presented.

Sense of Agency

How can we move away from feeling victimized toward a stronger sense of agency?

"Sense of Agency" is the term I chose to define what I consider the greatest self-management tool when faced with toxic professional situations. In essence, Sense of Agency refers to the level of awareness that we have about the possibility of impacting our own life or work environment.

"Agency" implies taking responsibility over the events of our lives, seeing ourselves as an "agent" of our own history, and not as a passive bystander. Its main constituent behaviors are shown in Table 4.11.

Table 4.11 Sense of agency framework

Sense of self	Sense of responsibility	Sense of choice
The extent to which we are aware of what belongs to us and what belongs to the perceived narcissistic leader, recognizing our own behaviors and those of others (intuitive understanding of transference and projection)	The extent to which we recognize the link between the quality of the relationship with the perceived narcissistic leader and our own behavior (opposed to thinking or acting as a victim)	The extent to which we recognize our reasons ("secondary gains") for remaining in the toxic relationship and freedom to take action

Very few people have both the strength and the capability to find meaning in hardship while in the midst of it. It is a lot easier to look back on your negative experiences once they are over, and then be able to take the appropriate lessons from the experience. When working in toxic environments, it would not be surprising to find yourself falling into the trap of feeling like a victim. In fact, you have all the right to feel like a victim in such situations—but it does not mean you cannot do something about it.

What is noteworthy in my research is that very few people recognized that there was something wrong going on right from the beginning of the relationship. Most of the interviewees were slow to differentiate between what belonged to them or to their leaders, hesitated to learn how to better deal with the situation, and continued to feel guilty. While people got more puzzled and confused, time passed by while the emotional and physical damage piled up.

A few points differentiated one person from the other, with regard to the awareness process. At first, there were three aspects that seemed to vary from person to person:

1. How long it takes for the person working under a toxic relationship to realize there is something wrong going on.
2. How long it takes for the person to recognize what he or she has to do with it and understand his or her responsibility in the process.
3. How long it takes for the person to be courageous enough to ask for help to understand, learn from, or better deal with the situation.

Another interesting point which emerged is about excessive resilience, which might lead people to persist without acknowledging the psychological or physical damage underway. Evidence of this can be seen in one of the interviewees who regretted not taking interesting job offers in the past, claiming her toxic relationship caused no harm to her professional self-esteem, for example. Still another interviewee experienced severe health problems before finally deciding to resign. Thus, enduring suffering is not always the best option, since trying hard to resist and survive may present a high bill to pay in the longer run.

There are a couple of cases that may be worth exploring before drawing some conclusions.

Five interviewees firmly stood their ground and confronted their leaders more "aggressively." One was transferred to another location. Another one survived by performing above expectations and putting together complex political games to protect herself. The other three seem to bring something new to this discussion. The first one would not pick up his boss's calls during the evenings or weekends, setting some clear limits to the relationship. The other two confronted their leaders by standing up for their personal values: one gave her boss a strong lesson about what is acceptable corporate behavior when discussing how he treated one of her subordinates; another one lost her temper and told her boss to call on her team only when she had finally decided to respect them.

One possible hypothesis is that whenever people are brave enough as to speak from their hearts and tell the truth, the authenticity that emanates from that "agent" in the situation seems to lead even narcissistic leaders to back off. However, speaking the truth may not be as effective if the narcissistic leader is not "well-intentioned." In this sense, the effectiveness of the strategy would greatly depend on the values and beliefs behind the leader's actions.

If we go back to our proposed definition of Sense of Agency, we can make the following assumptions:

1. **Sense of self:** The ones who presented a higher level of awareness and were able to recognize what was going on within their inner

theaters were better equipped to develop effective coping strategies. This seemed to be true also for the ones who needed help to make sense of what was going on. So, the critical issue here seemed to be the ability to recognize that "something is happening inside and around me," and not necessarily one's ability to make sense of what that is by himself or herself.

2. **Sense of responsibility:** Only a few interviewees demonstrated this level of awareness, being able to describe how their own ways of behaving were reinforcing the narcissistic leadership behavior. Most interviewees did not perceive the narcissistic behavior as a response to their own behavior. Thus, developing a sense of responsibility seemed a harder thing to do.

3. **Sense of choice:** In this case, what the data showed was that, although many of the interviewees did recognize their "secondary gains" for remaining in the toxic relationship, they unconsciously chose to build perfect excuses to justify not taking action. In this sense, they might prefer to "choose not to have a choice."

As for this last point, a few cases are worth noticing.

Three of the interviewees who demonstrated a stronger "sense of choice" seem to have done that for completely different reasons. One of them had a lot less at stake: her financial situation was settled, and she was not so enthusiastic about the power or status provided by her job. Another one was so value driven that she could not remain "silent" in the face of moral harassment. The third one was so emotionally stressed that she reacted impulsively.

Viktor Frankl brings an invaluable contribution to this topic by suggesting that our last inner freedom is to decide what shall become of us (mentally and spiritually). This "spiritual freedom" can be a driving force for the will to act.[39] This supports the assumption that adults may be able to take a stand against abuse regardless of the complexity of the situation they are involved in. In this sense, the key might reside in being aware of where the line that cannot be crossed is, so that the executive is left intact.

Do you know what is really nonnegotiable for you?

In terms of building a stronger sense of agency, the shift that needs to happen involves moving away from blaming the narcissistic leader for his or her bad leadership behavior and start asking oneself what can be done to be left intact, both from a psychological and physical perspective.

Now, would you agree that the need to build a stronger sense of agency goes way beyond narcissism and is a desirable attitude to effectively deal with crisis, change, and uncertainty?

Reflection and Awareness

Reflection and awareness are necessary steps to turn hardships into learning. But how does it work?

As said Saint Francis of Assisi: *"Lord, give me strength to change what can be changed, resignation to accept what cannot be changed, and wisdom to distinguish one from the other."*

There are things we can change, and others we can't. Crossing narcissistic leaders is not something we wish for. But since we cannot prevent this from happening, nor do we have the power to make them change, all we can do is to stop believing that they are the only problem. We can do something about it. When we truly want to learn and count on the necessary ingredients to do so, there is just nothing that can prevent us from growing and evolving, even in the face of adversity.

In this frantic world in which we are overwhelmed with information from all sides, we unlearn a fundamental skill: the ability to reflect. Reflecting is different from thinking. It is a deeper and more contemplative process of observation. It takes time and patience. It can often feel safer and less distressing to occupy ourselves in such a way that we don't have "time to breathe." Many of us are proud to say how busy we are. It adds status and prestige. Being busy seems to justify our existence, giving us the fake feeling of being indispensable. Reflecting, therefore, requires something we don't enjoy having: time!

Discovering our truth requires creating space for reflection. Those who live on autopilot mode do not have empty spaces that can be used to reflect. Reflecting is scary, because when we reflect, we end up seeing what we do not always like to see. On the other hand, we have a chance to discover that our greatest enemy, most of the time, is not outside, but within us.

What would we find out if we took the time to reflect about ourselves, our choices, and our life?

Another factor that may prevent us from reflecting is fear!

Increasing our awareness can be a painful process, despite how liberating it may be. Perhaps, that is why so many people would rather remain in the darkness. But this may not be a choice for everyone. It takes more than courage. It takes resilience to carry the burden of acknowledging our own imperfections and vulnerabilities, as well as a lot of determination to move forward, trusting that we can always better ourselves.

Now, if life challenges us with uncomfortable situations which allow us to develop skills that can be useful in the future, why not step up to the challenge?

Many of these situations can be worthwhile if they serve to make us stronger. While, on the one hand, suffering and hardship are undoubtedly unpleasant experiences to go through, there is hardly anything as impactful in terms of learning.

Another way to look at this is that, for some people (not to most of them, to be fair to the data), working with those narcissistic leaders also turned into a significant developmental experience, which led to a legacy of great accomplishments that they could be proud of throughout their professional journeys.

Seeing the narcissistic leader as an opportunity? What?

We are all in agreement about the destructive potential of such leaders. Unfortunately, however, there is very little we can do about it. Yet, we can try to understand the extent to which we allow ourselves to be manipulated and remain in toxic situations by our own choice. Dealing with pathological leaders is often a way of venting our own need to project our dark side onto others. It is a lot easier to blame others for our difficulties. And almost everyone will support us when we complain about our toxic leaders, making it harder to resist the temptation of placing ourselves as innocent victims begging for compassion.

By the way, just between us, is it not irresistible to badmouth a toxic leader?

All we have left is to try to understand our role in such relationships. So, once we have survived, maybe it was worth it after all....

Conclusion

We can look at toxic experiences such as working with narcissistic leaders as nondeserved misery—or as hardship that can help you learn, and even flourish. These strong negative experiences have the power to become life-changing if one is humble enough to realize that: (a) the complexity of the situation justifies reaching out for help no matter how resilient you are, and (b) behind every struggle lies an opportunity to reinvent yourself.

Facing the need to ask for help and dealing with our own vulnerability require courage. This is how we reaffirm our ability to reflect and expand our consciousness. Likewise, believing that we can always learn, even in the face of the greatest adversities, can be deeply liberating.

Reinventing yourself might not require a complete turnaround. Yet, a deeper dive into your inner theater will allow for a better understanding of the extent to which your own projections interfere with your ability to establish healthy professional relationships. In this sense, no matter how odd it may sound, a narcissistic leader may be an opportunity to come to terms with your own insecurities or even grandiose fantasies, setting you free to live a more genuine and purposeful life.

Working to change the narcissistic leader might not only be difficult but also extremely frustrating. Dealing with pathological narcissism is like "moving in quicksand"—the more you move, the more you sink. It is risky, scary, and potentially damaging.

Sometimes, the best you can do is to protect yourself. Moreover, trying to fix it may also reflect our own narcissism, which leads us to the illusion that we have the power to change other people, even against their will. On the other hand, when we fail in our attempts, we risk start feeding the little "victim syndrome" inside every one of us, instead of helping us build a stronger sense of agency.

So, if you are looking for a way to strengthen yourself instead of drowning in the narcissistic leadership quicksand, try looking inside yourself first, before trying to understand what is happening around you.

But, please remember that it is better not to walk alone, especially in unstable soil such as the ones contaminated by narcissism.

My purpose in this chapter, above all, is to shed new light on what can be done to survive the hardship of narcissistic leaders, by taking the advantage of these uninvited guests to create a better version of yourself. Learning and growing out of adversity is far from easy. It requires being both vulnerable and courageous at the same time.

So why not strive to recover your agency while trying to survive narcissistic leadership?

CHAPTER 5

Vilification and Its Impact on Senior Leaders

Ross Emerson

> *You learn eventually that, while there are no villains, there are no heroes either. And until you make the final discovery that there are only human beings, who are therefore all the more fascinating, you are liable to miss something.*
>
> —Paul Gallico

Opening Reflection

As a consultant working with board directors and senior leaders, I support clients facing a plethora of difficult and intense situations. My work comprises senior executive coaching, business consulting, and board advisory using a systems-psychodynamic approach in order to ensure sustainable impact at the personal, team, and organizational levels simultaneously. I first learned about the systems-psychodynamic approach while completing an EMC degree course at INSEAD. Since completing the program, I have become a staunch advocate and proponent of the approach. I integrate psychodynamic techniques and methods into my everyday work and I am continually surprised by the positive impact this has to effectively diagnose organizational problems and to identify challenges faced by senior leaders.

The systems-psychodynamic approach is particularly helpful during periods of crisis or during periods of transformation involving multiple organizational changes. Both these scenarios disrupt daily life for the organization and the people within it. This is accompanied by shifts in interpersonal dynamics and results in a great deal of organizational pain. Incorporating a systems-psychodynamic approach in my work enables me to quickly identify hidden challenges standing in the way of business success. Once these challenges are uncovered and brought to the surface, they can be addressed and resolved.

Introduction

When organizations experience crisis and change, the complexity and challenge can be overwhelming. In my work, once trust is established and psychological safety is created, clients begin to think of me as personal confidante with whom they are able to share their vulnerabilities. Through the stories I hear, and the coaching interventions I design and implement, I often acquire a different, somewhat unique lens on situations. What I find most intriguing is the impact of the specific situations on individual leaders themselves and how these affect their well-being in the long term. We often see these types of dynamics play out in current corporate and political landscapes. In business, for example, when companies are faced with cybersecurity attacks and breached firewalls, the CEO or Board is held accountable and the blame is often projected onto a person, not a position. And in politics, we witnessed these types of dynamics both before and after the UK Brexit vote in 2016 and in the lead up to the 2020 U.S. presidential elections. In more current times, we can see these dynamics through the COVID-19 vaccine nationalism that is visible on the global stage. As a professional supporting senior leaders through difficult periods, I take note every time I observe such dynamics. As these situations play themselves out publicly, I am continually reminded of the work I do with clients and the impact such occurrences may have on the person individually.

One senior leader I spoke to was accountable for a global restructuring of the firm where he held the role of managing partner. He had a professional obligation and responsibility to act in the best interest of both the business and its employees. During the transformation however, despite the best intentions he had to safeguard the livelihoods of people working in the organization, there were inevitably job losses and redundancies when a new organization structure was finalized and the optimal labor complement was reassessed. In such situations, senior leaders are often vilified by employees for the negative impact that results. Another senior leader I interviewed shared a story about a freak accident that took place on the property of one of the real estate holdings held in the company's portfolio. A visitor to the company ignored well-placed and highly visible safety notices and wandered into an unsafe area and had a horrible accident which left him paralyzed. Despite that person's own decision to stray into this unsafe section, the local community and media vilified senior leadership for the accident. The Chairman of the firm became the target of people's anger and was hounded for quite some time to the extent he had to step back from his professional role.

Well-intentioned leaders make decisions and act in the best interest of their companies when fulfilling their professional duties; however, they can never guarantee that things will go according to plan. Little consideration is given to the fact that these leaders are people—human beings susceptible to the same emotional and psychological scarring as everyone else. After months of working with senior leaders navigating highly intense situations involving crisis and change, I determined that they were experiencing severe difficulty and it could be argued that they were *vilified* by others. They struggled to make sense of the emotional, psychological, and often chaotic aftermath they experienced. Coaching work provided a new lens on the situation, revealing similarities between what they experienced and what trauma survivors experience as known and widely accepted by society. This inspired me to research the topic of vilification further. The questions I wanted to explore were "What happens to leaders at both the conscious and subconscious levels when they are vilified?" and "How do leaders cope when vilification occurs?" I started by reviewing scholarly literature and theory to see what had been discovered before; however, I could not find any previous research that could help me understand the experience of being vilified from *within* the person, the embodied, lived experience if you will, so I conducted my own fieldwork.

I chose qualitative research because it takes a descriptive and interpretive approach.[1] Qualitative research focuses on words, narrative, and texts as meaningful representations of concepts[2] to capture the essence of an experience.[3] A critical incident method was used to identify a particular event that triggered the vilification phenomenon. I used a research questionnaire comprising 25 questions, as well as live discussions and semistructured, socioanalytic interviewing. The questionnaire doubled as a tool to foster a guided reflection when recounting inner experiences and also provided a degree of structure and consistency for people who participated in the study. Employing a discursive, conversational, socioanalytical interviewing framework was the best way to get into the minds of the research subjects and to collect linguistic data for analysis and interpretation by getting below-the-surface to truly understand the experience.[4] To integrate the systems-psychodynamic approach, I used the concepts of listening to one's inner theater and using self as an instrument.[5] I examined the inner experience of vilified leaders by coding themes of information that surfaced as they shared their personal vilification stories with me.

The age range of research participants was 38 to 69 years old with the average age being 53.4 years old. The gender mix was 66.5 percent male and 33.5 percent female. Participants originated from North America, South America, Europe, Asia, and the Middle East/Africa regions and came from a variety of professional backgrounds comprising consulting, financial services, capital markets, legal, government, education, private equity, and leisure/hospitality sectors. All the recipients of the vilification perceived it to be *unjustified,* meaning that the vilification arose despite having made decisions to initiate a course of action that would be considered reasonable, logical, rational, and appropriate by professionals in most circles given the information available at the time. This chapter shares my research findings and discusses some practical applications and considerations of the insights gained.

The following case study is representative of all the research participants and provides an indicative illustration of the dynamics experienced:

Case Study

As Chief Operating Officer, I had oversight of all transactions in a firm that was operating in a highly regulated industry. I had left a similar role at a high-profile organization to join a smaller company in a neighboring town in the same capacity. I wanted to be able to spend more time with family. I initially joined as a consultant but was made permanent after identifying a number of key issues for the business and demonstrating strong knowledge and capability in the compliance and regulatory space. I was also the only member of the team who had the depth of knowledge required to navigate complicated transactions coming up. I uncovered cases of fraud that had started a few years prior to my joining the firm and subsequently led on all activities to identify the person responsible and uncover any impact to the firm's clients. The federal and regulatory authorities were notified as was required, and at one point during the investigation proceedings, I was asked in my role "How did this happen?" I felt my reputation was damaged, and this was the first instance I started to feel vilified.

Later on, my peers on the senior management team started to make negative comments to me, essentially accusing me of not informing them appropriately when I first started to suspect wrong doing. They spoke to me as though this was all my fault. I had no support from my peers or the President of the company. The situation got so bad that eventually I had to resign my post and agree to high confidentiality about the whole situation under a tightly worded separation agreement. Initially and for a while after, I felt at fault even though I had nothing to do with the situation. I took responsibility as per my professional obligation and my personal values system and work ethic. I felt hurt and stressed, but I was determined to see this through professionally. At one stage later on in the investigation when I noticed a change in how I was being treated, I started to think to myself "This is not going to end well for me."

I was being treated like a second-class citizen, no one was properly listening to me and I started to feel like they would never listen to me, and dynamics during our meetings changed. I began to realize through comments made and a change in behavior from other senior executives that they were starting to realize that they were screwed because I had lived up to my professional responsibilities, but nobody was listening to me and they had neglected their professional responsibilities. This has very serious implications in the highly regulated sector.

Eventually, I began to see that I was being made the scapegoat. As things progressed, I realized more strongly that things were not going to end well for me and that I was going to be thrown under the bus and blamed for any shortcomings in our firm because my role as Chief Operating Officer held the responsibility and accountability. I felt so let down by everyone and angry that they were going to pin it on me even through it had nothing to do with me and I was the one that uncovered the whole situation. I felt hurt; I started to blame myself, and I repeatedly was questioning what I could have done differently in the situation. I took ownership of the situation in my effort to help, but it ended up working against me.

On a scale of 1 to 10 in intensity, I would place myself at 12, way off the scale. I tried to get through day by day. I was already doing 10- to 12-hour days, but through this period, I was doing 14- to 16-hour days. I just had to get through it. For a while, I was questioning my career path and career choices, and at one point, I thought to myself that I never want to go back into this sector again. I felt for quite some time that it was my fault. I had a lot of self-doubt. I repeatedly questioned whether or not I did something wrong. It's been about three years since the incident and I still feel the pain as though I was living through it again. During all of this, my husband would say that I am taking on too much responsibility and trying to give too much to everyone. He was angry at how all of this was affecting me and was trying to help me see that I am not to blame. He would say I was very affected by the whole thing.

In my personal relationships, there was not much change. This is probably because I didn't really tell anyone except for my husband. I did not tell family as my father was diagnosed with a terminal illness and I did not want to add stress and pressure to my elderly parents. I had a sister but lost her to cancer previously, so I felt I had to keep everything to myself. Even the things I did share with my husband, I played down the reality so that I would not create stress for him too. I no longer expect others to do the right thing; I now realize that they will do what they think is necessary to protect themselves. Before I was the type of person who automatically trusted, and if you lost my trust, you would have to work hard to regain it; now I am still a person whose default is to trust; however, once you've broken that trust, you will never get it back regardless of what you do or how much time has passed. Only one chance at trust with me, and if you lose, it it's gone forever.

The image I have of what I went through was of me being thrown into a tar pit. I am at the end of my rope and sinking in the quicksand. I desperately wanted someone to throw me a lifeline. I think I was functioning as normal before, but during and after the incident, I'm not sure you could call it functioning. I was so consumed by the whole thing because of its seriousness and intensity. I also found that after the incident, I no longer get joy from the things that I really used to enjoy doing, like running or going to the gym. I find it hard to get pleasure from the things that once gave me pleasure. There was no support from my firm. I turned to my husband for support and a very small group of close friends as I was not able to speak about anything for legal reasons.

At the beginning, I was very confused, shocked, and in a bit of disbelief at everything that was going on and how I was being treated. Later, I felt hurt and let down but others. Now as time passes, I still feel very raw about the whole thing, but more and more, I get a sense of relief and my life is very slowly starting to turn around. At this very moment, I feel very upset. Sharing my story with you is like reliving it all over again and the intensity of what I went through comes rushing back. It's a bit overwhelming.

I really appreciate the opportunity to tell you my story; this is cathartic and I know it's a safe outlet for me. Aside from my husband, I don't think anyone else has heard as much detail about the whole thing and what I was feeling besides you. I may have even told you more than I told my husband because I was trying also to protect him from the true reality of the situation and the possible implications for us professionally and personally. One thing that this brings up for me is asking myself "what do I really want?" Do I want revenge? NO. Do I want affirmation?—YES, I want to heal and I think if I was approached by some of my former colleagues and just received a few positive words from them, even though it would not really be an apology, although that would be welcomed, it would be enough for me and it would really help me to heal.

Visible Dynamics Above the Surface
in the Realm of the Conscious

I observed 15 emerging themes through the review and analysis of questionnaires, notes from live interviews, and reflections on the researcher's own experience. These themes were then clustered and coded into five *meta-experiences*. I selected the labels based on the illustrative nature of what was encountered as interpreted by myself as researcher. Following this categorization, these meta-experiences were sequenced in the order they were observed.

Emotional State

The first of five meta-experiences observed was *emotional state*. This meta-experience comprises strong emotional responses/reactions after the triggering event, intense emotional and psychological stress, and long-term scarring emotionally due to the framing of experience through negative associated thoughts and feelings.

All leaders studied reported overwhelming feelings of shock, disbelief, confusion, and bewilderment. Even when some form of reaction from others was anticipated, a strong emotional response still occurred within the person vilified. The emotional reaction was immediate, and the impact was described as very intense. Participants were asked to rate the level of intensity on a scale from 1 to 10. In a minority of cases the ratings were below 8. In the majority of cases, the ratings fell in the 8 and above range. In one case, the interviewee rated the intensity level at 12, emphasizing the severity of the experience embodied. The language used, such as "I could not see a way out," or "an uphill battle with no way to win," or "the emotions were intense and debilitating" indicated intense emotional and psychological anguish.

The effects were long-lasting with a residual impact. Most participants admitted to having multiple episodes of the experience immediately and long after the incident. This took the form of recurring nightmares and flashbacks and resulted in physical strain, entering into trance-like states, emotional volatility and mood swings, difficulty sleeping, strain on personal relationships, and difficulty speaking about the situation to others for fear of being judged. When asked why this may have happened, most participants explained that they had been thinking about or had to talk about the incident in the period preceding. The situation was often described as reliving the event all over again. There was little or no access to support depending on the nature of the incident, the cultural norms in their communities, the time when it occurred, and the geographical location and this had the impact of elevating their distress. In few cases when support was available, a lack of trust owing to the support offered being closely connected to the company in which the participant was employed meant support was not taken up.

Peoples' inner moods were sometimes communicated through use of colorful imagery. A diverse range of associative images was spoken about, but water featured in many of the recollections given by interviewees. Some descriptions of their situations included "like a tsunami had hit me," "I felt like I was drowning," "a blemish or stain on my life," "a train crash," "a vampire in the shadows waiting to pounce," "at the end of my rope and sinking in the quicksand," "I desperately want someone to throw me a lifeline," "like a vice grip on my head," and "I am standing in a storm with winds so powerful as to destabilize." Dark or muted colors, such as black and gray, or images often associated with mystery, suspense, and horror were also present in the associations.

Impact on Relationships

The second of five meta-experiences observed was *impact on relationships.* This meta-experience comprises negative self-images, disappointment in constellation relationships outside the immediate family such as friends, peers, co-workers, and so on, and development of a fault-line mentality and splitting, often described as adopting a *me-versus-them* stance.

When their self-image was challenged by others during the vilifying event, participants felt abruptly and aggressively confronted. Self-confidence was lost and self-doubt emerged in every case as the leaders were reflecting and questioning their actions (or lack of) and thoughts about alternative courses of action that could have been taken emerged. The feelings of self-doubt persisted and were overwhelming throughout the vilification experience. One interviewee frequently referred to himself as an "imposter" throughout his live interview, while another interviewee had internalized an identity of a "con-man."

The situation the leaders found themselves in had a profound effect on key relationships, both personal and professional. They relied on their family and close personal friends occupying their innermost circle of trust. They shared their deepest thoughts and feelings of vulnerability more easily with these groups and also took solace from supportive comments that reaffirmed that they were not to be blamed, were not at fault, and had done no wrong. These close personal constellations provided psychological support, emotional refuge, and in some cases physical nurturing when no other channel could be accessed.

Once the initial shock was mitigated, there was an overwhelming feeling of disappointment in some of their closest professional relationships. The solidarity they believed had existed was nowhere to be seen, for peers and colleagues distanced themselves expeditiously. Some described the situation as "true colors being shown" in the fallout of the vilifying event. In every case studied, interviewees admitted to not being able to trust others as easily as before. Increased cynicism in professional constellations had set in and suspicion and paranoia regarding their interactions with others resulted in increased caution for purposes of self-protection being used as a new default. Participants started to have a bipolar view of others as either *with them* or *against them* and developed fault-line mentalities in relation to people outside of their closest trusted constellations.

Social Defenses

The third of five meta-experiences observed was *social defenses*. This meta-experience comprises dynamics used to protect oneself from others and includes reflection and introspection, isolation/secrecy/retreat/insecurity, and obsessive cognitive processing and formulation of new narratives of self.

All participants searched within themselves and reflected deeply on the situation to understand why they were being treated so horribly. There were harmful feelings of isolation and abandonment without support from others whom they expected to be sympathetic to their circumstances. Secrecy was either mandated or implied depending on the nature of the incident, and participants themselves chose to hide or downplay information about the intensity of their experience from close family members as a means of protecting loved ones in some cases. At a certain point, they all required safe space to help them cope with the situation. This requirement was fulfilled by retreating from the outside world or changing their socializing behavior—particularly in high-profile cases that captured media attention. They described the circumstances as "overwhelming" and delegated tasks to others where possible in order to minimize contact with those perceived to be hostile parties.

Coping mechanisms were triggered to endure the emotional and psychological stress they were in. These predominantly occurred in the form of replaying the incident in their minds, numbing of feelings and emotions, denial of the situation, avoidance of certain people, and inability to believe or refusal to accept what they were going through. Rationalization along professional terms was also used to a great extent to convince themselves that they did nothing wrong and were simply fulfilling their professional obligations. Mentalizing of the incident was used at times, as was attribution and projection of blame onto others. Many people demonstrated signs of memory loss or selective memory when questioned about certain details during the live interviews.

Conflict Management

The fourth of five meta-experiences observed was *conflict management.* This meta-experience comprises acceptance and acknowledgment, emotional and psychological containment, and spirituality and attention to personal well-being.

A key enabler for participants to move past the experience was making peace with the situation and developing the ability to contain and more effectively channel the emotional stress as time progressed. For incidents that took place long ago (> 15 years), the impact had lessened. But for recent incidents (< 5 years), they described the experience as very raw and painful. For incidents between 5 and 15 years ago, the situation was described as manageable but still painful. For incidents that continually occurred owing to regular duties of the professional role, the impact was described as expected but still jarring every time it occurred. Their ability to function normally was affected, negatively impacting their health for years after the event. Participants wrote or spoke about stress, anxiety, elevated heart rates, high blood pressure levels, lack of sleep, and the loss of appetite. They also spoke about both emotional and physical exhaustion. Meditation, increased spirituality, or turning to religion for comfort and calm were also cited as ways to manage and contain the inner turbulence through stressful situations.

Recovery and Healing

The fifth and final meta-experience observed was *recovery and healing*. This meta-experience comprises ongoing reflection and creating focus on well-being, a desire to heal, and catharsis.

Heightened awareness of the impact of the psychological stress on their well-being and health was an experience shared by all the people interviewed. They spoke of a strong desire to get back to normal life and move past the vilification experience. The suffering and pain they exhibited were indicative of surviving a horrible accident or unwelcome traumatic occurrence. The leaders contemplated what they needed to bring the negative experience to closure and move on—assuming that was possible—and in several cases, the words "recover" and "heal" were used specifically when this topic was discussed.

Participants reportedly needed a treatment to alleviate the pain they had lived through. They wanted to understand the situation from the other side's perspective. Some simply longed for acknowledgment at a human level of what they went through to be able to recover. Some of those interviewed hoped for a discussion to debrief after the event in order to make sense of and draw a line under it. There was widespread acknowledgement that the closure they seek may never come about, but they were confident the passing of a sufficient amount of time would enable them to move forward in their lives.

Gratitude to have the opportunity to *tell their story* was witnessed in every case, but recounting the events seemed to open old wounds and cause them to relive their agony. There was genuine thanks and appreciation for being able to share the experience from their perspective and the act of going through the sequence of events, in every case, reminded research subjects of key lessons for work and life, as well as the strength of their resilience and ability to overcome challenging situations. Telling *their story* helped to mitigate strong emotions and pain they still seemed to be harboring. Although the pain may take a long time (if at all) to dissipate, the intensity was alleviated through the sharing of their stories. They were able in time to bounce back from the situation they faced, although they will never forget the experience; this helped them gain more perspective about life and dealing with other people.

Following the vilifying incident, the research subjects also adopted different approaches to dealing with people and many admitted to subsequently focusing more on human dynamics in their workplace. Some looked back on their experience and concluded that different decisions could have been made, even though their original choices were not reflective of any wrongdoing. Routine changes also emerged, as well as more attention given to life balance in order to safeguard personal well-being. A compelling motivation to participate in this study by all those interviewed was to share their experience in an effort to help other people who may find themselves in the same situation. As some put it, they wanted to "pay it forward" to help others.

After coding the five meta-experiences, a second coding of the 15 themes was then done by stage of time stage that each emerged. These were categorized as *early-term, mid-term*, and *long-term stages*. There was no specific unit of time measured, but these labels reflected when in each participant's inner experience life cycle of the emerging themes occurred, as interpreted by myself as researcher. Although the *meta-experiences* were sequential, there was time-stage-overlap in many cases. For example, the emotional state meta-experience could have started and be in *mid-term* stage when the impact on relationship meta-experience commenced. Likewise, the managing conflict meta-experience could have started before the end of the *early-term* stage of the social defenses meta-experience. This can also be described as *layers* of meta-experiences encountered simultaneously in real time through the three time stages. Table 5.1 maps in summary the above-the-surface experience data gathered in this study.

Table 5.1 The above-the-surface lived experience of being vilified

Meta-experience	Early term	Mid term	Long term
Emotional state	Strong emotional response Strong emotional reaction	Emotional intensity Psychological stress	Long-term scarring/ negative framing
Impact on relationships	Negative relationship with self	Disappointment in constellation relationships	Fault-line mentality/splitting
Social defenses	Reflection/ introspection	Isolation/secrecy/ retreat/insecurity	Obsessive cognitive processing/new self-narrative formulation
Conflict resolution	Acceptance/ acknowledgment	Emotional/ psychological containment	Spirituality/ attention to well-being
Recovery and healing	Ongoing deep reflection	Focus on personal well-being	Desire to heal/ catharsis

© Ross Emerson

Invisible Dynamics Below the Surface in the Realm of the Subconscious

After mapping the lived experience, I shifted my focus to determine the below the surface dynamics causing this experience. In the following section, I first summarize the results of the critical analysis conducted and then proceed to unpack the hidden subconscious drivers.

Summary of the Phenomenon

Participants in this study *perceived* they were vilified by others. Because vilification was unjustified in their specific instances, their inner transitional experience was traumatic and painful with enduring emotional and psychological scarring. Above the surface, they encountered five meta-experiences of emotional states, impact on relationships, social defenses, managing conflict, and recovery and healing. These manifested through early-term, mid-term, and long-term stages. Below the surface, the perception of being unjustly vilified equated to being stigmatized. This activated a threat appraisal process to assess and confirm the presence of identity threat. Identity threat in turn triggered a state of cognitive dissonance. As participants transitioned through this deeply uncomfortable state, they experienced a variety of painful encounters through the early- and mid-term stages and went to great lengths to cope with the effects by using identity threat protection responses. As they started to make sense of things through the long-term stage of their transition, they recovered and healed from their traumatic experience by employing identity-restructuring responses. This facilitated the rewriting of their self-narratives by allowing them to transform from villain to hero in order to help others through the sharing of their experience of being vilified. Figure 5.1 illustrates both the conscious (visible) and subconscious (invisible) inner experience of leaders who have been *vilified*.

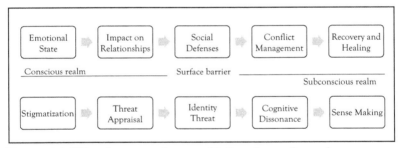

Figure 5.1 What happens above and below the surface when vilification occurs

© Ross Emerson

Stigmatization as the Trigger

Being vilified can also be described as being negatively judged or stigmatized. Stigmas discredit individuals and discount them. Stigmatization occurs when someone processes a social identity that makes them feel devalued. When participants felt vilified, they perceived this as a stigma, discriminatory in nature and devaluing and discrediting their personal social identities.[6] Stigma identity management has important social impact on a person. Deferring to stigmatization by concealing one's truth may inadvertently reinforce the stigma.[7] These perspectives assume that stigma puts a person at risk of threat to his or her identity, may threaten self-esteem, create confusion whether the stigma arose from one's personal identity or social identity,[8] and instill fear of judgment.[9] In this study, stigma's effects were witnessed through the lens of the receivers' interpretations of how others saw them, their perspectives of social implications, and their motives and goals. The motives of the stigmatized were impacted by how they perceived and appraised the situations. These motives included protecting or enhancing self-esteem and believing in a system that treats them fairly.[10]

Threat Appraisal

When stigmatization occurred, participants immediately entered a process of threat appraisal which involved assessing how harmful the stigma (perceived as *villain* in this study) was to the participants' self-identities, what responses will result as a consequence, and how this affects self-identity from that point on. The appraisal process is interconnected with models of psychological stress and coping,[11] as was evidenced through this research. The threats observed in this study most likely occurred from identity conflicts within the participants, that is, the tension between their values and beliefs of self-identity as contrasted with their perception of what being vilified meant for their identities. This was influenced by their own deeply embedded perceptions of what being a *villain* means, and its widely accepted cultural meaning of the embodiment of evil and something to be rejected.

Psychological stress and coping models describe five possible primary appraisals of an experience specific to identity. These include relevance to identity, preservation or benefit to identity, potential for gain/growth, harm to identity, and potential harm to identity.[12] This study revealed a dominance of harm to identity and potential harm to identity. The widely held negative views of participants meant the more likely identity threat would be confirmed, because it has to do with participants' perceptions of self, which are deemed high in importance.[13] People are more likely to address identity-related information when it pertains to an identity deemed to be important,[14] and the more an individual is exposed to an experience, the more likely it will be a threat because of its salience and difficulty to rationalize as an anomaly.[15] This was evidenced in this study in high-profile cases which pitted large numbers of people against the participant; and in organizational contexts where the participant was vilified by groups of people simultaneously due to situational circumstances such as company restructuring resulting in employment loss.

Identity Threat

Individuals value their identity and this sustains their self-worth.[16] Identity threat arises from one's subjective appraisal of an experience indicating potential harm to one's identity. *Primary* threat appraisal occurs when the impact to one's well-being is assessed; *secondary* threat appraisal occurs when potential responses to the threat are determined. The appraisal process is "integral to models of stress and coping"[17] and can be "automatic, nonverbal, instantaneous, and occur outside of the consciousness"[18] below awareness.[19] Appraisals can also occur by affective processing (i.e., feeling) instigated by culturally embedded cues.[20] Identity threats can originate from identity conflicts which arise between values, beliefs, norms, and demands inherent in identities.[21] At a high level, threats can also originate from beliefs and prejudices held by society—such as *villains are evil*. Threats are generally traumatic, can occur randomly, and are unique in that they are independent of specific individuals or groups.[22] When identity threats are detected, identity threat coping responses are activated and these could include *identity-protection responses,* such as concealment, or *identity-restructuring responses,* such as changing the meaning of the threatened identity.[23] Identity threat harms a person's self-concept[24] and members of stigma-induced identity threat groups have a greater risk of mental and physical health problems.[25]

Cognitive Dissonance

A state of cognitive dissonance was activated as soon as identity threat was confirmed, and this brought on a host of *identity threat coping responses.*[26] These are cognitive and behavioral with the objective of decreasing likelihood or severity of potential harm.[27] Threat coping responses are described in two categories. The first targets the source of the threat and is called *identity-protection responses*. These surface in three forms: derogation, concealment, and positive distinctiveness.[28] When a new identity is realized, the person momentarily encounters a period of surprise.[29] Once the initial shock had passed, coping mechanisms dominate to contain or deflect the harm. These identity-protection responses appeared in the early-term and mid-term time stages of this study. Participants had strong, protective emotional responses and found ways to isolate themselves, withdraw, or conceal the situation from others to preserve/maintain their previous identity, manage internal conflict, and find emotional and psychological safety.

Being vilified leads one to embody many thoughts and emotions that might be inconsistent with one's positive self-image. Such inconsistencies bring about the sensation of psychological discomfort, indicating the presence of cognitive dissonance.[30] Cognitive dissonance theory posits that "when one experiences such dissonance, it creates an unpleasant feeling that one will go to great lengths to alleviate."[31] New information contradicting self-image is often met with a combination of defense mechanisms and mental tricks. These are particularly powerful when the original cognition relates to positive self-image.[32] When an individual realizes they have done some harm to another, there are often "intense and disruptive emotions after enactment, such as guilt and anxiety." Realizing that they have hurt another person may also bring about a certain level of remorse and discomfort. Their behavior may also be justified to help align the conflicting behavior with existing beliefs. When this cognitive dissonance is experienced, a person will search for explanations and ways to minimize the uncomfortable feelings or attribute responsibility to someone else. When responsibility attribution is unsuccessful, the person will turn to other types of avoidance or active coping mechanisms.[33] Studies show that when it comes to self-concept and self-identity, "the facts and preferences are molded to fit one's identity as opposed to the other way around."[34]

The emergent themes and meta-experiences visible in the realm of the conscious surfaced in a sequential pattern through each successive live interview. This suggested that the invisible dynamics encountered in the realm of the subconscious also transpired in a sequential pattern. It was apparent that each of the participants experienced a high degree of discomfort from the mélange of intense emotional reactions encountered. These emotions were disruptive and indicative of an emotional and psychological maelstrom: an inner turbulence brought on by *cognitive dissonance*.[35] The presence of cognitive dissonance triggered a host of social defenses for self-protection and to help cope with the inner chaos.[36] The simple act of being vilified was internalized as a violation of expectation which resulted in doubt and a challenge of beliefs.[37] This conflict of values with deeply embedded self-perception created a painful and traumatic inner experience that required resolution. The situation confronted the participants and forced them reevaluate their sense of self to cope with feeling of self-doubt, guilt, confusion, shock, and so on. It also forced them to reassess their social safety nets believed to be in place. In most cases, this resulted in disappointment at the lack of support received, which increased their sense of isolation, vulnerability, and perceived threat. It fostered splitting, making participants feel that others were either *on their side or against them.* And the experienced pain and need for resolution became increasingly apparent through the turbulent time. While hearing about their experiences, I had associations of a sinking ship and of a surgery taking place in a hospital operating theater. The intense emotional and psychological stress further impacted mental and physical health negatively, thus compounding the discomfort experienced. Evidence of cognitive dissonance mitigation was seen in the attempts to justify the participants' roles in the vilifying event, described by many as fulfilling their professional obligations and duties of their role.

Sense Making

When a state of cognitive dissonance exists, a state of sense making usually follows. This is often seen as rational and intellectual processing through mental reasoning models. Sense making allows people to "enact (make real) their environments through social construction and committed interpretation" to achieve stability by means of justifications that mitigate confusion. It is the process by which people "label, categorize, and create plausible stories that retrospectively rationalize" what is happening. Sense making is sometimes "deliberate and coherent, but sometimes spontaneous acts of interpretation that create new meaning and narratives by perpetually drawing on past events and conversations."[38] In doing so, one recreates themselves and others as a way of moving on.[39] Sense making is also temporal, happening both in the moment by drawing on past experiences, present interactions, and future anticipations, and secondly occurring across time through a series of small, subtle, responsive, particular, in-the-moment, and often contested experiences. Sense making is undoubtedly embodied and entwined with identity.[40]

To alleviate their discomfort and make sense of things, participants in the study described being obsessed with finding some external cause for what happened. There was excessive cognitive processing, that is, mentally replaying of events continuously to figure out why the unexpected had occurred.[41] This was a rational process that seemed to consume them as they searched for alternate meanings and explanations. Forms of spirituality, such as meditation, prayer, and deep reflection, facilitated new perspective on the incident and perception of self. Memory suppression played a role in the rewriting of their inner self-narratives. Longer term effects were embedded in their minds, helping to stabilize the inner emotional and psychological chaos so that self-narratives could be rescripted as a way of moving on.[42]

Making Sense by Rewriting Self-Narratives

The identity-protection responses evolved to *identity-restructuring responses*, the second category of identity threat coping responses. These attempt to change an aspect of the threatened identity to make it less harmful and sometimes also to abandon or exit the identity altogether. Identity-restructuring responses enable the individual to change their threatened identity or the views of the source of threat. This impacts the appraisal process and has the potential to eliminate the identity threat.[43] Participants in my study started with withdrawal and isolation in the mid-term time stages but carried forward this isolation to the long-term time stage through the state of sense making. Participating in this research facilitated a kind of regression therapy; engaging in the research process was a way of making sense of their experience by allowing them to relive the event, rewrite their inner narratives of self-identity from villain to hero, alleviate their inner pain, and continue to heal. Identity-restructuring responses manifested through the participants' finding new meaning from their experiences and transforming their identities from evil to good—exchanging the negative identity of villain for the positive identity of hero—as a means of resolving the cognitive dissonance to make sense of things before moving on.

Storytelling as Catharsis

Participating in the research was cathartic for all the participants. Although the experience was emotionally intense, exposing their vulnerabilities and having the chance to *tell their story* was highly effective in helping them cope with the incident, reaffirm their personal learning and growth, deal with latent and residual feelings of shame, guilt, anxiety, fear, anger, and betrayal, and also to highlight their resilience and new perspective on life. This was particularly liberating to them given their earlier implied or self-imposed directives to remain silent during the time of the actual incident. In several instances during the sharing of their stories, I had associations of a bird flying out of a cage and of a prisoner escaping a jail cell. It was intriguing to observe how participants wanted to reframe their lived experience and transform themselves from villain to hero. Recreating themselves as the hero in line with their deeply embedded self-identities gave new meaning to their experience. This was one of the sense-making mechanisms used to mitigate the impact of cognitive dissonance experienced when vilification started. At the beginning of the research process, participants viewed themselves as unjustly cast in the role of the villain. Their motivation to help other people learn from their experience facilitated their collective transformation *from villains to heroes*—committing acts of selflessness for the benefit of others, in line with cognitive dissonance and sense-making theory.

Practical Applications and Considerations

Given the lived experience of being vilified, one can easily understand how resulting inner dynamics could affect leadership performance. The conscious and subconscious stages that vilified leaders transition through affect both the emotional and physical well-being of those who experience this phenomenon. This, in turn, could manifest in diminished capacity for good judgment, risk mitigation, human capital management, and strategic and critical thinking. Support for leaders facing these dynamics may be warranted and can be justified through both a professional and human lens.

The insights gained in this study transcend the professional and personal domains and are applicable to the business world and the helping professions. In the professional domain, better organizational training programs could be developed by incorporating the findings of this study to prepare those in business who may themselves be in this situation and also to prepare those who are called upon to provide support to these individuals. This can also be said for those in the close constellations of the vilified—such as family, friends, colleagues, managers, and HR teams—in order to help people in this situation cope better through the experience and reintegrate to business- and life-as-usual quickly and effectively. In the personal domain, better understanding the impact of being vilified could enable those in the helping professions, for example, executive coaches as well as other types of therapists and support providers, to be more effective in their roles. The catharsis theme, in particular, comes to mind as it was noted by all research participants that sharing their story, although emotionally charged and difficult to do, helped in the recovery and healing process and enabled them to reframe a bad situation and use it to bring about some good. By shedding light on this topic society as a whole can be better prepared to address the outcomes through the lens of well-being, which is increasing in importance in both professional and personal circles.

This study can also be of benefit to professionals who are more focused on learning, development, and the manufacturing of bespoke therapeutic or learning programs to help people overcome challenging situations where intense blame could potentially be present. These might include design and development of corporate led programs, self-help programs, self-help literature, and group therapies. This study has implications for organizational leadership at the highest echelons as well as HR functions within organizations. Executives need to be aware of how these situations affect their employees, regardless of level, and ensure that the appropriate support programs are available and accessible when needed to support their employees appropriately. All of these can be put to good use to help people dealing with this type of crisis to effectively cope with the situation in order to move past it, recover, and get back to life as normal. This should resonate with those at executive level because they are often the ones in the direct line of fire, forced to take accountability for the outcome when things don't go to plan, regardless of their direct involvement. And the same can be said for those in governance functions operating at Board of Directors level. Evidence of this can be seen easily in both business and politics for example. In the business context, we are witness to the implications for senior executives who may be lambasted and tried in the court of public opinion for the many shortcomings and negative effects of large corporate culture. The same can be seen by politicians deeply entrenched in state negotiations, for example, the controversial Brexit withdrawal negotiations, or alternatively the very public dynamics of (perceived) COVID-19 vaccine nationalism. It really does not matter what role or level of seniority one holds, being treated like a villain, and its consequential impact, is a widespread phenomenon that warrants deeper understanding. For HR functions, the insights suggest that targeted support programs can be developed or at the very least more easily accessible to employees who find themselves in these circumstances. Rather than having a punitive mindset toward them, perhaps a more compassionate, humanistic approach is called for, void of judgment and subjective opinion. Furthermore, awareness of the lasting impact can be integrated into leadership training programs focusing on developing emotional intelligence to encourage people to refrain from summary judgment and better understand the situation from all sides before jumping to any conclusions.

Coaching Insights

Executive coaches can learn from the insights and use them to tailor their coaching engagements accordingly. Better understanding the impact of being vilified enables executive coaches to be more effective in their roles. Insights can translate into more meaningful interactions for both the coach and the client. From the coach's perspective, the insights enable focus for the topics of the interventions, tailoring of the coaching approach, and adjustment to the pace of work to better support clients. They foster a common vocabulary between coach and client which improves the framing of issues, so clients can make sense of their experience, accept it, contain it as needed, cope with it over the course of the coaching work, and eventually move past the trauma and start to heal. Clients could use the insights to better communicate their experience to family, friends, colleagues, and so on by putting words to the feelings, emotions, thoughts, and overall psychological state they are in—both to share their experience and mitigate feelings of isolation and to ask for specific support when needed, such as the space to be alone with ones' thoughts, or the help of specialized professionals such as counselors.

The first major benefit of the insights gained comes at the contracting stage. As a coach, having a better understanding of what the client is experiencing informs the decision to coach or not. The insights could help coaches determine if this is an engagement that should be accepted or not. On the surface, this might sound a bit harsh and evil in itself—denying help to someone seeking it—but bearing in mind that not all coaches have the same training, background, experience, and capability, this decision whether or not to work with the client is for a greater good ... the protection of both the client and the coach. If the coach is not adequately qualified to work with client facing these issues at both above and below the surface, then the outcome could be detrimental for both parties. This implies that coaches who work with clients in these situations should have some psychological grounding to draw from such as psychoanalytic informed training for instance. Having a deeper understanding of the intrinsic dynamics enables coaches to assess the situation more accurately at the outset and make better informed decisions about working with a particular client, or if necessary, referring them on to an appropriately qualified helping professional.

As a second contribution to the coaching profession, the insights from this study may encourage coaches to pay closer attention to the emotional state of the client and more consciously look out for emotional triggers or situations where containment may be necessary. Recognizing the emotional intensity the perceived villain has experienced facilitates a more sensitive and extended trust building stage of the coaching journey, acknowledging the impact the experience has had on the client's relationships with others and resulting breakdown in trust as was observed in all the research participants. This trust building is critical for a successful outcome of any coaching program as it fosters open and honest dialogue between coach and client.

A third benefit to the coaching profession is heightened self-awareness of one's own internal dynamics through the client interaction. For example, coaches may have found themselves in the same situation as the clients they are working with. On the one hand, this can boost the relatability factor between client and coach. On the other hand, a similar experience to the client may also affect the coach's neutrality and objectivity, and potentially has implications for transference or countertransference[44] emerging through the coaching work. Understanding the dynamics at the outset can help coaches to better prepare to remain at the boundary and perform their role more effectively.

Conclusion

This research showed that circumstances examined may be more complex than what is visibly observed above the surface. The study recounts the lived experience of vilified senior leaders from the perspective of the vilified people themselves and reveals the resulting emotional and psychological impact. Through the lens of well-being, participants in this study could legitimately be categorized as trauma survivors; however, little support was available and accessible because deeply embedded social and cultural views about villains mean they are seldom supported, but more often blamed. With imbalanced systemic forces influencing people's interpretations of what is really transpiring, one can easily consider the *system as the villain*. The system further complicates recovery by perpetuating the silence and isolating victims, reinforcing the stigma by compelling them to keep things in the shadows rather than heal by sharing their stories.

Deeper reflection suggests that this study could also have been about the shadow side of judgment—judgment of others and judgment of self—and how it has the potential to emotionally scar and cause long-term psychological damage. Stigmatization of others through a one-sided lens has the power to destroy. It creates emotional turbulence, and traumatic inner dynamics which are deeply disruptive, threaten identity, and negatively impact both mental and physical well-being. These dynamics are often invisible and impede the availability and accessibility of much needed support. This experience could either strengthen one's resilience, or at the extreme, damn one to psychological oblivion. In light of this knowledge, should we as human beings, capable of compassion, more often be asking ourselves the question, "Are the villains sometimes also the victims?"

> Judgment is a dangerous thing. It can lead us to misconceptions and error, to lose sight of things that may transform the image altogether. For some, judgment may lead to undeserved elevation or help them find a strength they didn't know they had. For others, unfairly placed or premature judgment can lead them on to their destruction, or to hurt and destroy others. We cannot change the mistakes that made these people what they are or distorted their reputations beyond recall. We can however do them the justice of thinking before we judge and giving them the understanding (Blakeney 2010, n.p.).

CHAPTER 6

The Reflection in the Paper

Reducing Anxiety and Increasing Self-Reflection

Ricardo Senerman

Introduction

Knowing yourself is the beginning of all wisdom.

—Aristotle

On what makes a leader: The first thing I look for is emotional intelligence—basically, how self-reflective is the person.

—Manfred Kets de Vries

Chronic stress, according to the World Health Organization, has reached epidemic proportions. Although less visible and less immediately deadly than the devastating COVID-19 virus, chronic stress is responsible for a series of physical medical disorders and symptoms, and serious mental health problems. Perhaps, the demographic group with the highest stress level is corporate executives.

Contributing to the level of stress in executives, which according to multiple reports has reached crisis proportions, is the intense performance pressure of today's corporate world. A working paper from the National Bureau of Economic Research, for example, found that executives look older and die younger because of the high stress of their jobs. And the job is not getting easier. While COVID-19 impacted the mental health of individuals in every profession and work situation, another study found that high-level executives suffered more intensely from the pressures of the pandemic than their employees.

The crisis of executive stress is not just a health issue; it also impacts leadership performance. Indeed, the ability to pause and reflect, to know one's inner self, and to regulate and express emotions is a core trait of leadership. Unfortunately, the challenges of leadership positions make time an extremely limited resource and busyness one of the defining features of a CEO's life. In fact, in a recently published study of more than 400 top CEOs throughout the world, 48 percent acknowledged that they require and would benefit from periods of personal reflection. Yet, while those leaders fully recognized that reflection is essential to their roles, many admitted that finding such time is very difficult.[1]

The emotional impact of the busyness that typically defines the CEO's life is often overlooked. Busyness has the capacity to act as a particularly attractive manic defense mechanism, suppressing what one is really feeling and what is most troubling. By staying busy we are able to keep at bay feelings of loneliness, depression, and, above all, the anxiety of death.[2] Information overload is an important factor acting as an enemy against pausing and paying attention to our inner world.

Busyness and chronic stress also lead to burnout, which researchers define as "a toxic mix of exhaustion, reduced professional efficacy, and increased cynicism about work that research from Gallup suggests affects about two-thirds of full-time workers at any given time. ... Executives, however, aren't usually aware of their stress-related patterns and idiosyncrasies and often don't realize the extent of the stress burden they are already carrying. Leadership stereotypes don't help with this. It's no surprise that we can't articulate how stress affects us when we equate success with pushing boundaries to excess," wrote Jan Ascher and Fleur Tonies in February 2021.[3]

In short, finding the time for reflection is becoming more and more urgent as impact of stress, burnout, and emotional issues such as chronic anxiety on executives is reaching crisis proportions.

To make things even more difficult, few executives are willing to embark on a psychoanalytical inquiry or even ask for professional psychological help. The motivation for excellence that makes a person climb the corporate ladder comes from a tendency to be somewhat narcissistic,[4] so recognizing flaws and listening do not come naturally. Reflection does not come easily for "high achievers accustomed to leaping into action to solve problems."[5] There is also the perception of weakness that prevents many executives from recognizing or seeking solutions to their psychological stress. This may result from "the imposter syndrome," which really stems from a sense of insecurity. If you are insecure, you are hesitant to betray any weakness.

Furthermore, the real challenges and stress associated with top management positions today is sometimes difficult to understand for people who have not participated in the turmoil of corporate life. Professional coaches can certainly help, but many times they lack sufficient experience to work with top-level executives, and/or they are expensive and difficult to find. Executives realize they need more time-efficient systems, and they need to perceive them as more effective and manageable than traditional responses to stress and turmoil. They are beginning to understand that if they are able to find such methods, "they can free themselves from their psychic prisons."[6]

Executives are also realizing that gut feelings and emotions are becoming essential tools for increasing effectiveness. "Greater self-awareness is the first step toward becoming a more effective leader ... a willingness in self-exploration—that first essential step in the process of personal change—is a sine qua non for people in responsible executive positions."[7]

I am among those who have become a victim of the pervasive stress of the life of an executive. I have participated in start-ups, fulfilled multiple executive roles, and am presently serving as a CEO, Chairman, and Board member in several organizations that have a significant public presence and are sensitive to many stakeholders, including public scrutiny. Through these years I have felt my fair share of anxiety and other stress-related issues. I have sought various ways of coping, including meditation, exercising, hobbies, writing, and even medication, along with receiving various types of external support, such as coaching, psychological systemic therapy, and years of psychoanalysis. I can say from my experience talking with others in similar roles that I am far from alone in this quest.

This experience, and the realization that most people in leadership roles share both the need for coping with anxiety and severe time restrictions due to their responsibilities, led me to ask if there might be a way to address these challenges in a simpler and more effective way that would not depend on specialists or medication.

With that question as a backdrop, I began to examine a number of proven methods used to improve psychological well-being. These include body scanning and *interoception* (interpreting what our body is telling us), affect labeling (identifying and naming our emotions), journaling, and expressive writing (EW)—all of which had shown great promise when employed separately. This further prompted me to wonder if mixing or combining such methods within a single system would be worth examining. Could such alternatives, tied together in a single methodology, serve as a simple, but effective vehicle for self-therapy? Might there be some synergistic benefit from mixing them? Could a person, on his or her own, employ this solution and still achieve meaningful results—that is, some measurable relief in symptoms together with meaningful insights into his or her inner life?

These questions led to the development of a therapeutic system for accessing and addressing emotions that I present in this chapter. This system, which I called the Deep Emotion Expression and Processing (DEEP) System, builds on extensive psychodynamic research, including research into the importance of expressing your feelings in words (affect labeling); the newer approach of moving past emotional defenses to uncover the core, internal feelings driving anxiety; and the recent advances in neurobiology and the relevance of body awareness and interoception.

The Theoretical Origins of DEEP

Since Freud's famous depiction of the analysis of Anna O. by Dr. Breuer, the value of expressing emotions has been fully acknowledged. In his *Studies of Hysteria*, Freud documents this first case of a cure achieved by expressing repressed traumatic experiences and the related emotions, which resulted in the birth of psychoanalysis.

> For we found, to our great surprise at first, that each individual hysterical symptom immediately and permanently disappeared when we had succeeded in bringing clearly to light the memory of the event by which it was provoked and in arousing its accompa-

nying affect, and when the patient had described that event in the greatest possible detail *and had put the affect into words.*[8]

Today, there are several branches of psychotherapy that have developed from the original "talking cure." The work in this chapter has been influenced by what is referred to as the short-term psychodynamic psychotherapy approach. This approach is focused on achieving results in the short term, in contrast to the long-term mindset of traditional psychotherapy, and calls on the therapist to take a more active role in the therapy sessions. Rather than just sitting and listening, therapists using the short-term psychodynamic psychotherapy approach will challenge and engage with their patients, helping them plunge into the deep emotions at the root of their problems. Such an approach was chosen because, while having its origin within the psychodynamic model, it provides faster results (see below). The short-term approach has been proven to be "significantly more efficacious than other therapies on anxiety at both posttreatment and follow-up"[9] and has several systematic ways of treatment that could be applied to the DEEP System.

It was Sandor Ferenczi, a disciple of Sigmund Freud, who started experimentation with a more active approach in psychoanalysis. He was the first to put an emphasis on emotions over interpretation. This is one of the marks of what came to be known as the "Budapest School." Alice and Michael Balint, disciples of Ferenczi, moved to England and in turn had an impact on David Malan, who became convinced that dealing with emotions was more important than making interpretations, such as the interpretation of dreams for which Freudian psychotherapy is known.[10] Malan developed what he called the Triangle of Conflict,[11] which demonstrated how defenses (D) and anxieties (A) block the expression of true feelings (F) (Figure 6.1).

The objective is to consciously recognize the emotions, also known as core emotions, at the bottom of the triangle.

As humans, we are aware of the conscious part of our lives, visible and obvious like the tip of the iceberg, but ignore the vast, unconscious part of our lives below the waterline. However, what happens in our unconsciousness—the core feelings that reside there—intrude into our consciousness, poke at us, and push us to raise our defenses. In my case, for example,

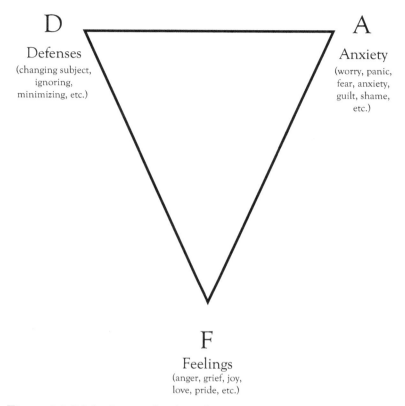

Figure 6.1 Malan's triangle of conflict

Source: Adapted from: Affect-focused psychodynamic psychotherapy for depression and anxiety through the Internet: A randomized controlled trial.[12]

I know I use procrastination as a defensive maneuver: I will avoid thinking about an unpleasant (scary) task with a certain deadline until the last minute (it goes without saying that I suffer by postponing more than by doing, but it is a nonrational process). In more drastic cases, people will turn to drugs, alcohol, and other defenses to push away the core feelings they want to avoid. Or they may become obsessive about a certain activity, even a healthy one like going to the gym or even jogging for several hours a day—anything to avoid addressing the core feelings that disturb us.

The truth is we cannot hide from ourselves no matter how hard we try. The core feelings that we learned in our childhood that were "inappropriate" remain with us. For instance, if a boy is told that he shouldn't cry, he will bottle up emotions that might bring tears, keeping them below the water line but always totally present, commanding his actions. Our well-being depends, however, on surfacing those emotions, accessing them, and dealing with them, which requires making the time for self-reflection and self-compassion. We need to come to accept and recognize who we are, regardless of what was deemed acceptable by our early caregivers in our childhood. This does not mean that we can always act on our emotions, but just to acknowledge that they are present goes a long way toward a better quality of life.

Emotional Processing

"The recognition of defenses and getting past them in order to access emotions are the *sine qua non* of psychodynamic psychotherapies."[13] The need to stop, or at least reduce, the avoidance and repression of thoughts and feeling is clear. The avoidance has effects contrary to what the person wants, ironically *activating* them below consciousness in a "deep cognitive activation process."[14] This is what makes mental control ineffective.

In developing an emotional processing system to address the crisis of stress and anxiety in executives, starting with myself, I needed to create a flexible therapeutic routine that would lead to self-reflection and the discovery of core emotions.

I eventually focused on two effective approaches: *interoception* and *expressive writing.* Interoception refers to the process of recognizing the emotional signals that your body may be trying to send you (think of how you sweat when you are nervous). A proven methodology for interoception consists of a deliberate "body scan"—focusing intently on all of the pains, discomforts, and pressures that you feel in your body. These may be muscular, postural, related to inner organs or skin, such as heat or cold, upset stomach, tight neck, and breathing speed and depth.

In the following section, I describe interoception in more detail, followed by an in-depth description of the second approach, expressive writing.

The Body Keeps the Score

Antonio Damasio, in his book *Looking for Spinoza: Joy, Sorrow and the Feeling Brain,*[15] dethroned Descartes famous "Cogito ergo sum" (I think, therefore I am), and recognized Spinoza's approach toward an indivisible mind–body connection.[16] "The division between reason and passion, or cognition and emotion (an opposition that goes all the way back to Aristotle), is, from a neurological point of view, a fallacy," mentions a *New York Times* article aptly named "I Feel, Therefore I Am."[17] Work by Damasio and Carvalho reinforces this view of an inherent link between body and mind:

> Whether feelings portray an internal state (hunger or thirst) or are prompted by an external situation (for example, compassion or admiration), their dominant mental contents describe a state of the body in which the conditions of the viscera (for example, heart, lungs, gut and skin) have a key role.[18]

In other words, when we are very fearful, the mind is thinking, "I am very afraid" but is also aware that the heart is beating furiously.

When seeking insight into the body's inner dynamics, the concept of "interoception" has been proposed. Interoception can be defined as a process in which "the nervous system interprets, and integrates signals originated from within the body to provide a moment-by-moment mapping of the body's internal landscape across conscious and unconscious levels."[19] Physiological processes often ascribed to interoception can be painful, such as headaches, joint pain, bruising, or nonpainful, such as fatigue, hunger, sensual touch, respiration, and vasomotor flush. Some features of interoceptive awareness include observing internal body sensations, perceived intensity, and differentiation from other sensations. There have been various models that link dysfunctions of interoception with mental illness. Furthermore, psychiatric disorders have symptoms and signs that are related to interoceptive dysfunctions. For example, general anxiety disorders display such symptoms as headaches, fatigue, gastrointestinal issues, muscle tension, as well as such signs as sweating, trembling, nausea, and an exaggerated startle.[20]

Several approaches to trauma processing and healing also relate to emotion and body states. Among them is "Somatic Experiencing," developed by Peter Levine, which is geared toward resolving chronic or posttraumatic stress by primarily directing attention to interoceptive and proprioceptive sensations, rather than to cognitive or even emotional experiences. (Proprioception is the ability of your body to know its location in space, which is why, e.g., you can walk without looking at your feet.) As Levine explains, "It is the body's narration that therapists must address in order to understand physical and visceral reactions and to mobilize them in transforming trauma."[21]

In our daily activities, we often have to subordinate our feelings to the task we need to accomplish. For example, our bosses may need something urgently, we may have an issue with our kids at school, or we may have lost an important bid related to our business. In such cases, our reaction must be subdued and we have to "maintain our cool" so to speak.[22] If the connection with the body is lost, the person is left in a state of dissociation, which prevents that person from making sense of her or his experience.[23] Nevertheless, as Van der Kolk's bestseller book title expresses: "The body keeps the score."[24]

The Power of Expressive Writing

A pencil is one of the best of eyes.

—Louis Agassiz

I can shake off everything as I write; my sorrows disappear, my courage is reborn.

—Anne Frank

The virtues of writing as a tool for personal development have been long recognized. As Van der Kolk explains, "Writing has particular benefits. ... You are free to go into a sort of a trance state in which your pen (or keyboard) seems to channel whatever bubbles up from inside. You can connect those self-observing and narrative parts of your brain without worrying about the reception you'll get."[25]

Walter J. Ong, a Jesuit priest and Harvard PhD, is recognized not only for his work and books but also for his lectures at Yale, Cornell, and other universities. His interesting Opening Lecture in 1985 at Oxford was in fact entitled, "Writing is a technology that restructures thought."[26]

Just labeling an emotional experience reduces emotional arousal.[27] The possibility of confession, long used by several religions, relieves the burden of keeping secrets and reduces or eliminates the costs of suppression and inhibition, which ironically can lead to activation of the suppressed emotions. This might well be related to the detrimental effects of inhibition that has been studied by a range of thinkers, from Freud to Wegner. In contrast, as James W. Pennebaker, developer of the expressive writing method, explains, "The reduction in emotional sensitivity that follows from disclosure of emotional events[28] might also be traced to the movement from deep to full activation—and perhaps from there to no activation at all." Thus, while attempts to suppress emotions only make them stronger and more persistent (i.e., they are "activated"), expressing such emotions serves to quiet them down. As Sparrow and Wegner note, "There is evidence that expression of any thought lessens its recurrence."[29]

Expressive writing (EW) has been shown to reduce anxiety and enhance well-being by allowing people to express stressful life experiences and, at the same time, promote self-distancing—in short, "looking from the balcony"—and meaning making. This process, often referred to as emotional processing, allows people to reflect on past negative experiences without becoming overwhelmed by the emotions associated with them, in a way that serves as a buffer against rumination and getting stuck in trauma. This is because the "self as narrator" is separated from the "self as protagonist."[30] The technique employed in EW is usually for participants to spend four sessions of 15 minutes each writing their deepest thoughts and feelings about a traumatic experience.[31]

A great deal has been written on the power of EW and its relation to affect labeling (putting feelings into words). Emotional writing in general lessens the recurrence of subsequent unwanted thoughts.[32]

Affect labeling has been proven to improve emotional and physical health. It "diminishes the response of the amygdala and other limbic regions to negative emotional images."[33]

> Affect labeling may enhance outcomes by increasing exposure to one's own fear and anxiety. Such a process may be similar to mindfulness, in which one becomes more aware and accepting of ongoing experience, and for which data support its relationship to improved psychiatric outcomes.[34]

EW can also encourage increased awareness of emotions, requiring clients to put feeling into words (i.e., affective labeling). Participants in EW tests have shown that repeated EW encourages reflection, and this in turn predicts positive change, even when they are not explicitly asked to modify their behavior.[35]

Not everyone benefits, however. Those who are seriously ill or had no disturbing issues benefitted the least. It seems that people moderately impaired by their problems seem to benefit the most.[36]

There is, nevertheless, much still to be investigated. Pennebaker[37] recently argued that the most important agenda for researchers in the field of experimental disclosure is "to find out when [experimental disclosure] does and does not work and with whom."[38] On disclosure and writing, among other techniques for escaping from thought suppression, Daniel Wegner writes,

> These assembled solutions for unwanted thoughts should be taken as hypotheses and possibilities rather than as trusty remedies or recommendations. I offer them in hopes that further research and exploration will discern whether they are indeed effective and that, in the interim, they may be useful to those who are trying to overcome unwanted thoughts, both in research and in everyday life.[39]

Even Pennebaker acknowledges that,

> We still don't know what types of writing instructions work best, who is most likely to benefit, which biological processes are most affected by writing, or what the best timing of the writing is. If you are interested in EW, experiment on yourself. See what works, drop what doesn't. And come up with some of your methods that are beneficial for you.[40]

From Theory to Therapy

EW has been demonstrated by more than 145 studies and meta-analysis to consistently improve mental, physical, and general well-being. It has even been proposed as a low-cost treatment alternative to more formal modes of therapy.[41] As I researched a therapeutic approach to relieving, through reflection and routine, the stress and anxiety of the lives of executives, I quickly realized that EW would form the core of the system I would develop. In time, however, I recognized the importance of integrating body awareness. Focusing on the fact that we exist in the real world as a physical body puts our thoughts in context—specifically, that our thoughts are *happening* to us. For example, if we are caught in the rain, we know that rain is happening to us because we feel the raindrops on our body. Our bodies are separated from the rain. By focusing on our body, we can separate our thoughts from our physical manifestation and realize that a thought is something that happens to us, like a raindrop, rather than something that we cannot separate from our body, like our height.

I thus created a new therapy, which I called the DEEP System that combined body awareness phase with a written exploration of felt senses and emotions, as an effective way of acquiring a more reflective and less anxious approach to work and life.

To test the effectiveness of this new therapy, I decided to use myself as the initial "guinea pig"—an approach I know has significant limitations, but also practical benefits. By serving as the initial subject, I was able to experience firsthand the merits and flaws of the approach, as well as the difficulties associated with execution.

This decision was not taken lightly. Due to time limitations associated with the research, I set as the standard timeframe approximately two months of writing with a frequency of four or five times per week and a minimum of 15 minutes for each session. It was a demanding task, requiring persistence and patience. Seeing that in all the studies reviewed there were several participants who did not complete even the three sessions required, I concluded that it would not be wise to try to recruit multiple people to participate in a controlled study that would require consistent near-daily writing over a two-month period; so I decided to test the effects of what I eventually called the DEEP System on myself. The resulting approach carries with it elements of the autoethnographic style, portraying my personal experience in multiple episodes, from which I tried to discern the patterns that appeared throughout this sequence.[42]

In addition, I employed Grounded Theory, "focusing on a process or actions that has distinct steps or phases that occur over time."[43] My idea was to use the data to expand on a theory that I deemed an appropriate design to use in this case, since although literature does exist on the topics studied, in particular EW, there have not been samples of longer term exercises on these matters. Also, I was piggybacking on Pennebaker's recommendation on studying *methods that prove beneficial to you* (see above, emphasis added).

In the following section of the chapter, I will detail the step-by-step process of the DEEP System (see Figure 6.2).

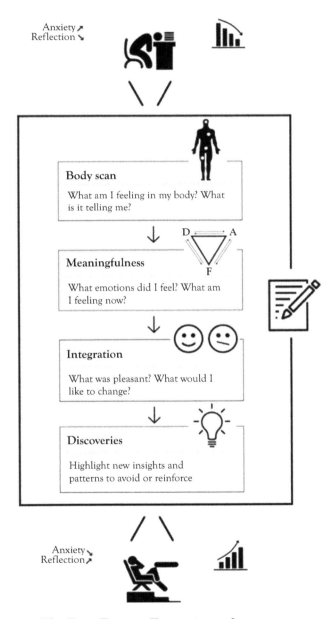

Figure 6.2 The Deep Emotion Expression and Processing (DEEP) System

Begin With the Body

In the first part of a session, I usually conducted a 5- to 10-minute scanning of my own body. "What am I feeling IN MY BODY?" I focused on becoming aware of my respiration rhythm and depth, shoulders position, temperature sensations in different parts of my body, awareness of skin feelings, gut sensations, muscular tension, and so on. I also looked for associations ("Mmmm, pain in my left wrist … any other pains?"). With each scan, I sought out at least 15 issues. I closed on that number after trying for up to 25, which I realized took too much time, and around 10, which did not allow me to quiet my mind enough to start the next section. Identifying 15 different body sensations took close to 5 minutes, and that was long enough: I did not want to use all my writing time on this topic.

The body scan had a particular effect. It took me away from the "out there"—the past or future, and centered me in the "here-and-now." It embodied me. Furthermore, the mere noticing of these many body sensations served as an introduction to "listening" beyond "hearing." As I explained earlier, listening to the narration that the body is telling us has been the essence of a whole area of medicine and psychology devoted to trauma. In this simple way, by paying attention to my body and viscera, I can "thaw" what had to be frozen during the day, when I had to constrain certain reactions such as fear, hate, or joy, depending on the situation and context. Through this process, the dissociation that happens by my accommodation to societal and particularly working environment can be dissolved, and a space for reconnection and acknowledgment occurs. As per Levine, Van der Kolk, and others who have opened the road to healing trauma by listening to the body, I can attest that even in the lack of severe traumatic experiences, the reconnection with the body is a pathway for reflection, well-being, and reconnection with self. I realized after this period that we are not brains on a tripod, but a full body–mind system, that, when taken care of and properly acknowledged, can release the body's stress and numbness; provide valuable information; start a beautiful conversation of mutual appreciation (mind–body); and foster gratitude and compassion within ourselves.

The possibility of finding a secure space through reconnecting with my body in the present, and then lovingly and respectfully listening to my organs, senses, and feelings, anchored me in the here and now.

Excerpt 1

> ... Tense jaw, neck pain, warm feet, shallow breathing (I breathe deeply, pleasurable feeling). Itch in right chin (beard hair), tired muscles around eyes. I feel a gentle breeze on my back, the cold table where my hand is resting. Pressure in grabbing the pen, the friction between my hand and the paper ... full stomach, curved back, shoulders tight and raised (I lower them) ... sigh, now a more relaxed stance, tinnitus, the touch of the shirt against my back ...

Expressive Writing Plus: A New, Structured Method

After 5 to 10 minutes of writing focused on body sensations, I moved to free writing with a focus on feelings, reflecting on emotions that were significant in the moment, regardless of when they had happened and their positive or negative connotation. This stream-of-consciousness type of writing is the standard method for EW, and it worked well, at least initially. My experience confirmed what Pennebaker himself had discovered: within four writing sessions, EW can bring intensive change that sticks; after the fourth session however, the improvement plateaus. EW is still therapeutic, but the increase in positive emotions and decrease in negative emotions does not continue trending upward and downward, respectively.

As a result, after one month of testing the traditional EW way, I decided to add more structure to the method to boost the effectiveness of the system. While I continued the body scan, which I found to be particularly effective with slowing down and "going to the balcony" to achieve a more reflective stance, I added *meaningfulness* and *integrative processing* to the EW exercise.

Writing that focuses on *meaningfulness* involves writing about the deepest emotions and most significant thoughts regarding events since the last writing (usually a day or two ago).

Integrative processing consists of reflections about the events and emotions that came up in writing related to meaningfulness.

In particular, I would conclude my writing sessions with descriptions of what had made me happy and energized me, and what drained my energy that I might want to change.

It is important to keep a log, to be used later for the *discoveries* section, which represents the last section of the writing (see below). This is the only part that should be kept for later reference. All the rest can be saved or discarded as needed. This is important because it allows you to download everything that comes to mind in your free writing part, since there is no need to keep it for later. You can even burn it if you want but do keep the teachings: things that are worth remembering and are significant in how they influence your mood and well-being. In this part, I transcribed or summarized with certain words, phrases, or short paragraphs the "aha" moments of the day's writings.

The creation of this four-part structure—the body scan plus the three-part writing and reflection steps fully described below—dramatically focused and enriched the EW exercise.

Meaningfulness

In the first of the writing sections, I concentrated on writing about the most significant thoughts and deepest emotions I felt during the day, or since the latest writing session. This was not a recollection of events, but an exercise in letting out, initially, what was pressuring my mind in terms of either anxiety (mostly) or elation (less). I also wrote about the situations that I considered the main events of the day, and the thoughts and emotions related to them.

Fundamentally, I entered the **Triangle of Conflict**, through the Anxiety corner (see Figure 6.1). I became aware of moments of the day in which I had been nervous, anxious, or reactive—moments that generally robbed me of my well-being.

After a few sessions, I realized that many of the stressful moments, and a few of the passionate ones, were the result of what can be traced to scripts, developed in early childhood to perceived consequences of interactions, that have not been contextualized or actualized.[44]

I realized the pervasive effect of transference, its impact in my life, and how it affected those around me. I sensed the profound affect that transference and countertransference plays.

Transference involves "actions toward people in the present based on models of the past."[45] Through reflection (and therapy or coaching based on the psychodynamic approach), "we can recognize past patterns that have been carried unrevised to present relationships and by becoming aware of them, increase the chance for adaptive change."

Countertransference is manifested either by turning away (boredom, indifference, forgetfulness) or activation, such as experiencing attraction, rescue fantasies, or even sexual desire. The power of these elements in our present life is inevitable. But the possibility of increasing awareness of their existence and their influence can at least diminish some of their grip on us and our relationships.

The DEEP System facilitated a slowing down effect on my flow of thoughts and feelings, adding detail and granularity. I had the feeling of stilling the water of a pond, so that I could see more deeply and become aware of the stones and weeds in the bottom. Another association that came to me was that of waterskiing and speed. Imagine diving off a boat into the water. The water is soft: as you hit it, the water parts and lets you in. Now imagine that you are waterskiing on that same body of water. There is a certain velocity at which the water turns almost solid: you're not only able to ski over it, but if you fall and hit the surface of the water, you can hurt yourself as if you were hitting a hard surface. Slow down and the water "changes" again, returning to its previously "soft" state that allows immersion without pain.

The DEEP System allows you to stop careening through life at water-skiing speed, helping you instead to slow down, go deeper, and discover what lays below. As I was engaged in the DEEP exercise, I was able to realize several aha moments. I suddenly began noticing, for example, how often I was having reactions that did not fit what was actually happening in meetings with other stakeholders in the office. Instead, repeating scripts from my youth, I was reacting to other people or situations from my past that had repeatedly made me feel scared, threatened, or ashamed. I noticed how, for instance, in some of these meetings I turned into a small, threatened child, worried about the consequences for not acting in the appropriate way that had been drilled there at an early age by my parents or other (supposed) caregivers—a transgression that could mean failure and punishment, just as it had in childhood. My inner "shoulds," a legacy of the past, were driving my actions and reactions today.

Integration

After going through writing the parts on body scanning and the main thoughts or emotions since the previous session, I would proceed to reflect for 5 to 10 minutes on what emerged from the writing. I focused particularly on those aspects that were pleasant or that I liked most, and on those about which I did not feel so good, and felt I could have done something different in the same situation. I realized that in many cases what I felt in those moments were either reactions to interactions, inner dialogues, and strong feelings generated by memories of inner dialogues in my past, or a fear of conversations and actions that hadn't come yet but loomed in an imagined future (many times catastrophic). As Mark Twain stated: "I've lived through some terrible things in my life, some of which actually happened."

My recollections of the day I was writing about were of both kinds, good and bad. I learned about the moments, actions, and internal dialogues, as well as the people or situations, when I was feeling joy, enthusiasm, or gratitude—which strengthened me. I also discovered situations and reactions that made me feel scared, weak, and angry. I learned that too many of my moments of anger were ultimately anger with myself. I realized a part of me was berating myself, for not reacting better, for not being smarter, faster, and so on. I discovered that generally it was not my own voice, but usually the voice of one of my caregivers that had made an outpost inside my head! It was here that I discovered a sort of passage through time, where the different incarnations of myself—me as a kid, as a young adult, or at other stages and situations of my life—were connected by a strand that went from the past into the present. I realized that I was panicked to feel again certain emotions of my infancy, and that I had somehow been kidnapped from the present into another life and situation, where I did not have the tools, or even the distance that I could now afford. The adult in me dissolved in these situations, and, as if I were hitting a panic button, an emergency system took its place and reacted with a "war-time script." These were defenses, such as acting out, projections, and other behaviors that helped me escape the anxiety felt in view of an essential "terrifying" and almost unmentionable emotion. I was surprised by the speed of the transition from a rational, centered adult to the desperate defensive child.

Through these moments of integration and making sense of the emotions of significant events, I also realized some social defenses that were being used by my working teams to avoid confronting the reality of our situation and our own responsibility in it. It took several discussions and hours of meeting before the "aha-moment" came. "They," the others, were not entirely to blame, but there was a lot that we could do regardless of stakeholders' positions. Since it was easier to blame someone else, however, we delayed acting on what needed to be done. Confronting our own fears and demons is no easy task—whether as individuals or in groups.

Discoveries

This was a process of rereading and highlighting what I had written for a couple of minutes, underscoring or copying parts of the session that I thought and felt were either new things, "aha" moments, or repeated patterns to either enforce or avoid.

In short, I found that I could develop a reflective stance, which transpires in a silent parallel way that is, however, available to intuition and perception. This attitude, this sort of distanced view (from the balcony), made me keenly aware on my own feelings and what is being not openly said or written. A relaxed and attentive stance fosters observation, facilitates entering a reflective space, allows the emergence of associations in a nonjudgmental way (even by our own internal judge), links conscious and unconscious elements by resisting defenses, and allows deep emotions to be sensed, accepted, and understood. Through re/reading and highlighting, patterns are discovered and brought into awareness to finally understand links between actual behaviors and reactions due to underlying emotions.

For example, let's take the body scan that opens the process, and see how it might lead to a discovery. At the beginning of the writing process, you describe how your back hurts, your shoulders hurt, and your elbows hurt. This pain is not new, and you conclude that it's the price of getting older. In the final phase of the DEEP System, as you ponder on these pains you described earlier, you realize that the problem is sitting in an uncomfortable chair. A chair may be a small thing, but you realize the impact that it is having on your well-being and comfort. You realize— you discover—that there is no reason to accept this painful discomfort and you refuse to go on as before. You have made a small but important discovery: having a comfortable place to sit and work is a way to improve your physical, and therefore your mental, feeling of pleasure—or at the very least, diminish your discomfort. You get a better chair, and you feel even better because you acted and advanced toward your well-being. A few simple discoveries like these and you will begin to feel objectively and measurably better.

The entire DEEP exercise can take as little as 15 minutes, although I found that there is a sweet spot at 25 to 35 minutes that, repeated three times a week, allows for the four stages to develop in an unhurried, pleasant way.

Pulling all these elements together, the expanded EW process, which I call The DEEP System, unfolds as follows:

The Writing Process: Writing Tools and Rituals

During the period I developed and tested the DEEP exercise, I became aware of the importance of choosing the right tools and developing a writing ritual. Due to the nature of the analysis, this is a very personal account, but I believe that it offers insights on the internal processes and preferences that an individual may encounter in trying an exercise similar to this.

I experimented with several methods and tools for writing. I started by typing on a computer to be better able to record everything being written. I soon realized that using a computer had a detrimental effect on "letting the flow go" in my writing. I was not only concerned about the writing but also about the many red underscorings appearing in the screen due to misspelling many words. Typing was, for me, obtrusive to the flow of my thinking and feeling,

Eventually, I settled on the use of a fountain pen and A5 size of paper—traditional tools that became for me, the most unobtrusive way to write from 15 minutes to 1 hour, without physical or intellectual exertion and while concentrating on feelings and emotions. I also discovered that cursive handwriting, in a slightly bigger size than my usual writing and clearly readable, was what yielded the best results for depth of reflection.

I also wrote in my native language of Spanish to allow for a more natural rendering of my thoughts and emotions.

Writing by hand had a very important effect on the kind of "journey" into which some sessions turned. The writing itself became invisible, and a soft but clear conversation among several parts of me and even others started to take place. There was a speed (slow), depth (profound), and lack of judgment that opened a door to inner parts of my psyche. It was as if a curtain parted, and a deep conversation with different selves and other beings happened, allowing for new discoveries and realizations.

Excerpt 2

> Writing with this pen is a pleasure ... almost like an art form. It is my writing, my way, with a flexibility, a nature-like analogue, not digital process. This way of writing is a bit of a trade, the work of my hands, personal experience and life; unique, more craftsmanship than technique, a work more of a trade than of a profession. It gives me peace, pause ... I like the connection with the real in handwriting.

The act of writing became a ritual, a little ceremony like the Tea Ceremony in Japan.

The use of a comfortable size and quality of paper, a fountain pen that would write smoothly, even an ink of a pleasant color and wetness, all became part of a pleasurable setting. Filling the pen, opening the notebook, writing the date and time, became part of a setting that would initiate a dialogue with myself, a journey within. Ritual serves as a valuable introduction to an inner journey.

I wrote five times a week, allowing for exceptions and rest, ideally on nonconsecutive days so as to keep regular track of the significant events and emotions associated with them over the last day or two. I also sought to write preferably at a set time, generally at night after dinner and before going to sleep. In this way, I would not have any restrictions like meetings or other work-related interruptions.

Excerpt 3

> I feel a certain pleasure of writing in a way that has been done for hundreds, if not thousands of years … I enjoy the feeling of the touch of the paper caressing my hand. It is simple but pleasurable. The flow of ink, seeing how it dries after a few words. It is becoming one with the paper. Paper and ink, thanks to this 'art of writing', have become one. No wonder certain cultures value calligraphy as an art …

One last point: I discovered that one of the keys to successful EW is confidentiality. After trying several methods for keeping a record of what was written, I realized that several of the topics that I had put on paper were of an extremely personal type. The mere fact that I was saving them for later review, or even worse, for sharing with other researchers, precluded me from writing my innermost private emotions and feelings. I finally opted for a personal promise not to share or save any parts that were "too hot to handle." I realized that, as Garcia Marquez said: "everyone has a public life, a private life, *and a secret life*" (emphasis mine).

I am convinced that in order for the DEEP System to work properly, the "therapist–client" confidentiality, in this case what is written without filter or fear due to a confession-like secrecy, is a must.

Testing My Progress

In order to provide some objective assessment of the impact of the DEEP System, I incorporated in my experiment the Positive and Negative Affects Schedule (PANAS), developed by David Watson and Lee Anna Clark in 1984. This tool offers one of the most widely used scales to measure mood and emotion (although Watson and Clark use the term "affects," for the sake of clarity, I will use the more common word "emotions" when referring to this test). In the PANAS test, positive emotions reflect the extent to which a person feels enthusiastic, active, and alert, while negative emotions refer to feelings of distress and displeasure, reflecting anger, guilt, fear, and so on. Both positive and negative emotions were designed to be relatively pure markers of either—that is, the emotions were carefully chosen so that there was little overlap between the different emotions.[46] It is easy to administer the PANAS test, which includes 20 questions—10 for positive emotions and 10 for negative emotions—that are presented in a particular order (Table 6.1). For the purpose of clarity, I present them in positive and negative columns.

By adding up the scores of each positive and negative emotion, you calculate an overall score for positive and negative emotion, as shown by this test taken on January 29, 2019.

PANAS has been shown to "possess adequate psychometric properties in a large sample drawn from the general adult population" and to provide a "measurement invariance across gender."[47] Thus far, it has been used in several studies related to EW.[48]

For this study, I used PANAS before and after my 50 writing sessions over the two-month period of the experiment. This provided me with significant quantitative measures of the impact of DEEP on positive and negative feelings.

In one writing session, for example, the total positive score before writing (BW) was 30, and the total positive score after writing (AW) was 41. Thus, the writing session improved my positive emotions by a score of 7.

Table 6.1 Test results

Date: *January 29th, 2019*   Before Writing: *30*

Time: *22:50*   After Writing: *X*

#	Feelings/emotions Positive	Score	#	Feelings/emotions Negative	Score
1	Interested	3	2	Distressed	2
3	Excited	3	4	Upset	2
5	Strong	4	6	Guilty	1
9	Enthusiastic	3	7	Scared	2
10	Proud	4	8	Hostile	1
12	Alert	1	11	Irritable	1
14	Inspired	3	13	Ashamed	1
16	Determined	4	15	Nervous	2
17	Attentive	2	18	Jittery	1
19	Active	3	20	Afraid	2
Total positive score:		30	Total negative score:		15

I was interested not only in the changes before and after writing for each session but also in changes that happened in my perceived emotions over time. The PANAS data allow this to be done in a more rigorous way than just a broad subjective appreciation of emotional trends. The first step was to calculate the total positive and negative scores for each session. In the example above, the total positive score was 74 (30 + 41). I then charted each session on a graph to illustrate the trends for each set of emotions over time. Figure 6.3 shows the trend lines for the two months of the experiment. During that period, the increase in total scores for positive emotions was 35 percent, while the decrease in negative emotion scores was 45 percent. The specific positive emotions that showed the most significant change were determination and enthusiasm, which increased 60 percent during the test period, while among the negative emotions, hostility was reduced by 60 percent. The reduction in hostility meant that my "short fuse" was getting longer!

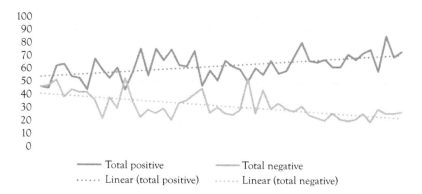

Figure 6.3 Data Trends

The increase in positive affects was 35% (in 2 months of 5 writings per week)
The decrease in negative affects was 45% in (same period)

One sees that the positive emotions keep rising steadily throughout the experiment, while the negative emotions keep decreasing steadily, proving unequivocally the effectiveness of the DEEP System.

During the same two-month period with five writing sessions per week, my mood swings (which can be calculated from the PANAS scores) decreased by 30 percent.

Although these results are not valid for everyone, they are significant and worth mentioning.

It's important to note that during the first half of the period covered in this chart, I was using the traditional EW method, that is, general stream-of-consciousness writing without DEEP System's separation into meaningful, integration, and discoveries writing sections. As shown in the graph, the traditional approach yielded a steady increase in positive emotions and decrease in negative emotions—that is, an overall improvement in well-being. Despite this initial significant improvement, the increase in positive emotions and decrease in negative emotions *continued* when I refined the approach into the four-step DEEP System. This indicates just how powerful the DEEP System can be. A parallel example would be a sick person feeling much better after taking some medicine, and then feeling even more significantly better after switching to another medicine. One wonders what the impact on the sick person would be if he or she had begun with the second medicine—just as one wonders what the improvement trend lines would have been had I started with the four-step DEEP System from the beginning.

The DEEP System at Work

Since developing the four-step DEEP System—body scan followed by a short three-step writing exercise—I have encouraged my coaching clients to undertake the process. Here are three examples (all of the names and some of the details have been fictionalized for the sake of confidentiality) of clients who have benefitted from the DEEP System.

At first glance, it seems that Julie, a successful and independent executive, should have everything to make a happy life. Coming from a family of traditional farmers, she was the first to receive a university education and has leveraged that degree into a thriving career that she loved. She also loves the vibrant city in which she works. And yet, she cannot shake a certain anxiety and unhappiness that hovers constantly near the surface of her life. Everything changes when she begins regular sessions of EW—short sessions that focus on surfacing the emotions she feels during the day. Using the three EW steps in the DEEP System, she writes on the meaningful moments in the day, reflects on the emotions felt in those moments, and, after rereading what she writes, identifies the discoveries or aha! lessons she can take from the session. Very quickly, Julie recognizes what is holding her back: her accomplishments mean nothing to her family, who believe that a successful woman is one who is married and has children. As a result, every time she talks to her family or visits with them (her hometown is not very far from the city in which she lives, so family visits are frequent), she feels as if she is drained of all energy. Her funk lasts for days. Eventually, Julie realizes that she has to focus on what makes her happy—the hectic environment of a big city and the thrill of her independent working life—and to reduce the guilt trips back home. When she has the opportunity to accept an executive position overseas, Julie does not hesitate. She leaves her country and moves to New York City, where she lives today free of the anxiety and stress that had once plagued her, and remains continuously energized by the city that never sleeps.

Another client of mine is a professor in his 30s who has no tenure and is stressed about the changes going on at his university. As he explains, "I feel so uncomfortable. I see that people less capable are getting on faster tracks. What I teach (management) is much needed and I love it, but it is not a hot topic. The stress I feel about the future and my growing family is too big." While engaged in the DEEP writing process at his desk, he sees the scale models of cars he collected—many of them assembled by him. He realizes that making scale models makes him feel an "unexplainable happiness" when completed. After rereading the part of this "discovery," he decides to take on a difficult engine assembly. He takes on this project. It has taken him weeks and is still not finished. His situation in the university hasn't changed. However, his relationship with his wife and little son has. He is happier, more patient, and even thinking about helping a start-up as an external pro bono director.

My final example involves a business owner in his late 50s. He has owned this business with a partner (and friend) for more than 20 years. However, the business is not going well. "The discussions we have with my partner are getting nowhere," he explains to me. "The business is in a dire situation. Our points of view are so different that we are pushing and pulling among ourselves while our managers are frozen without clear guidance!" Once he begins the DEEP System, he discovers that he is petrified of having a crisis with his partner, and that he will end up in court and lose everything that he has worked for. After a few more writing sessions, he discovers that his fears are enlarged by only seeing the worst. He realizes he is catastrophizing. He starts to ask himself, "What if things did not end in such a bad way? What if I could just mention the possibility of buying or selling my partner's share?"

He works on these thoughts and discovers a soft approach for starting the conversation. On paper, he is energized by the idea, but he drags his feet. After a few weeks, however, he feels worse because he is not acting, just writing about it. He invites his partner to lunch and cautiously drops the idea of splitting. The partner is relieved. He was thinking about the same lines. They easily strike a deal with my client buying out his partner for a small amount plus a reasonable upside bonus if the company succeeds. At our last conversation, he is still in difficulty but thrilled about being the sole owner and finally able to make the changes he believes will save his company.

Although these examples are drawn from my work with coaching clients, it's important to emphasize that the DEEP System is a psychodynamic tool that will help executives uncover *themselves* the underlying emotions that drive their energizing positive emotions (happiness, inspiration, etc.) and energy-draining negative emotions (anxiety, fear, etc.). Only the insights that come from within can be fully accepted and acted upon. Instead of hearing a third party declare, "Here is the answer," executives in crisis have to arrive at their own discoveries, at their own understanding of what they are feeling, and what is truly transpiring to elicit such emotions, good or bad. Self-discovery is ultimately the way to wisdom.

CHAPTER 7

Closing Remarks

Elizabeth Florent Treacy, Theo van Iperen, James Hennessy, Fernanda Pomin, Ross Emerson, and Ricardo Senerman

At the end of conferences or interventions with a systems-psychodynamic approach, it is common practice to take some time to review the work that has been done. In the spirit of group reflection, each one of us has contributed a closing remark, collected here as a kaleidoscope of themes or insights that we believe are important.

Harnessing Systems-Psychodynamic Awareness

The red thread in this collected work can be summarized by the phrase "there's more to it than meets the eye." Although the dynamics of crisis and change manifest at many different levels simultaneously, most people focus on what can be seen and try to ignore to the unseen. However, management of adversity is most effective when the organization can develop awareness of itself. A systems-psychodynamic approach to managing crises and change helps people in organizations to work with the realities they see *and* sense. This means that people are able to seek out and work with undercurrents that are less visible. They see the light shining under the door, through the dark.

Crises and change are most often framed as *events* to be managed by strategic planning or punctual interventions. This more operational approach neglects the emotional turmoil provoked by periods of disruption. Most change agents are aware of this emotional component, but they focus on the solution itinerary rather than the lived experience. Why? It may be that they are psychologically naive, believing that action is the best solution for emotional confusion. It may be that they fear waking the sleeping bear—potentially powerful or destructive emotional forces. It may be that they cannot recognize or work with their own anxiety.

However, to a greater or lesser extent, everyone in an organization is a change agent or crisis manager. The role may be formal, or unrecognized, or even rejected, but each person—and their emotional response to adversity—is influential in some way. Psychodynamic thinking brings into focus the emotional and symbolic aspects of individual behavior and decisions. A reflective change agent or leader models the ability to work through his or her own emotions; to consider what patterns or dynamics he or she is being "invited" to participate in; and to be open to interpretations and associations.

The ability to think systemically is another essential skill for leaders and change agents because they are always confronted with ambiguity: whereas a clear vision and consistent leadership actions are important, effective change management also involves the ability to explore what is actually going on, at multiple levels, in contrast with what was expected or intended. This brings essential data to light and fosters the courage to redirect the process if necessary.

Coping Strategies for Crisis and Change

The five chapters of this book describe different organizational and individual experiences of dealing with crisis and change. We have seen that complexity in times of great adversity translates into increased levels of anxiety, guilt, shame, and fear. It is like being lost in a giant labyrinth, while surrounded by a fog of emotions.

While this assemblage of studies on hidden challenges in dealing with crisis and change examines a variety of organizational settings, groups and individuals, collectively they suggest several key practices.

First of all, as the systems-psychodynamic lens reveals, the obvious solution is rarely the only one, or even the right one.

Second, organizations, and particularly their leaders, need to acknowledge that organizational life—be it virtual or in a physical place—is a shared space of profound feeling. Humans are far more than rational beings, and most of the stress, pain, and conflicts we experience at work tap into our deepest emotions regarding our sense of ourselves and relations to others.

Third, to begin to deal with these challenges, they must cease to be unspoken and instead brought into the open, where they can be named and productively discussed. This requires an atmosphere of psychological safety—whether it be in the organization, between bosses and employees (leaders and followers), or even within ourselves—where emotional risks can be taken without fear of rejection or reprisal.

Fourth, a single leader, or even a top executive team, cannot solve everything; on the contrary, a bottom-up approach increases real possibilities for profound change. From the organizational perspective, recovering after a cumulative crisis, or succeeding in a phase of transformation, requires collective leadership.

Fifth, consider what happens in organizations over time. There is richness in our history and our hopes. The concepts of nostalgia and postalgia deepen our engagement with the concept of slow-motion change. Stories shape the culture of an organization and hold important data. Listening to them helps an organization let go of idealized fantasies of past and future, and understand motivation or stuckness in the present. This is true for individuals—leaders and followers—as well as for organizations.

Finally, and most important for enabling the previous points, individuals must cultivate the practice of self-reflection across all organizational and individual levels. This is especially urgent when coping with the volume and speed of information that increasingly crowds out our ability to pay attention to our inner lives. It is almost counterintuitive: "Don't just do something, sit there!"

At the system level, organizations can also engage in reflective practices. For example, the leader may create for the group a regular space of review. In this space, the leader reflects out loud—sharing her own feelings of being curious or overwhelmed. She wonders where those emotions are coming from. She summarizes what she is hearing from the others, without judgment or intent to act. In such a way, she diffuses or steps away from the dynamic that is fueling anxiety. She models the playful space; she shows she can contain anxiety; she accepts ambiguity; and she shows her own vulnerability. This encourages each group member to recognize and be responsible for his or her capacity to accept or reject what other members in the group are saying or doing. Hence, ambiguity and emotion become distinct objects that a team or group can explore within the context of the external turbulence that is affecting them. This helps leaders and groups to recover a sense of calm. Over time, this helps leaders and teams to mature to a level where they are more aware of their own anxiety and can manage the emotions of the group as being distinct from the challenges they face.

Final Reflections

Organizational life was once framed and dominated by the school of thought that casts people in organizations in the role of economic agents, striving for their own best interest. While this perspective might have been valid at an earlier point in an industrial-based society, this book recognizes that organizations are social communities, not economic machines.

The systems-psychodynamic approach acknowledges that individuals in organizations share a fundamental human need to be respected and to contribute. By developing an empathetic awareness of the hidden undercurrents within organizations, we can better understand what motivates or discourages people. Far from being a process of manipulation or a vector of group think, this "habit of awareness" aligns people authentically with their roles and helps them make individual and system-level decisions that they can live with. In times of crisis or change, it is a strong protective factor against chaos and destruction.

Each chapter in this book showed us how diving into the unsaid and the unseen can help organizations not only to manage adversity but more importantly to prepare and live with all the unpredictable events that we are sure to face. We hope this book has inspired you, the reader, to experiment with team reviews, reflection, candid conversations, writing, and challenging your own perceptions about the people you work with. Together, we can live through adversity in a way that strengthens rather than depletes us—individually and as players in organizational life.

Notes

Foreword

1. Professor Erik van de Loo and Professor Roger Lehman are founding faculty directors of INSEAD's Executive Master in Change program.
2. Long and Harney (2013).
3. Lehman and van de Loo (2016).

Chapter 1

1. Stacey and Mowles (2016).
2. Fotaki and Hyde (2014).
3. Yerushalmi (1992).
4. Neumann and Hirschhorn (1999).
5. Carr and Gabriel (2001).
6. Suchman (2011).
7. Arnaud (2012).
8. Petriglieri (2020).
9. Carr and Gabriel (2001).
10. Arnaud (2012).
11. Fotaki, Long, and Schwartz (2012).
12. Fotaki, Long, and Schwartz (2012).
13. Kets de Vries (2001a).
14. Kets de Vries and Miller (1984).
15. Bion (1989).
16. Petriglieri and Petriglieri (2020).
17. Carr and Gabriel (2001).
18. Arnaud (2012).
19. Arnaud (2012).
20. Kets de Vries (1991).
21. Fotaki and Hyde (2014).
22. Hwang and Lichtenthal (2000).
23. American Psychiatric Association (2013).
24. Volkan (2009).
25. Petriglieri and Petriglieri (2020).
26. Yerushalmi (1992).
27. Kets de Vries and Miller (1985).
28. Kets de Vries (2009).

29. Kets de Vries (2001b).
30. McDougal (1985).
31. Etchegoyen (1991).
32. Kets de Vries (2006).
33. Luborsky and Crits-Cristoph (1998).

Chapter 2

1. Coldwell, Joosub, and Papageorgiou (2012).
2. Coutu (2002); Kets de Vries (2002).
3. Romanelli and Tushman (1994); Zaleznik (1997).
4. Kahn, Barton, and Fellows (2013).
5. Hannah, Uhl-Bien, Avolio, and Cavarretta (2009).
6. Pearson and Clair (1998).
7. Pearson and Clair (1998).
8. Hwang and Lichtenthal (2000).
9. Hwang and Lichtenthal (2000).
10. Beer and Nohria (2000); Marks and De Meuse (2005); Watkins (2009).
11. Beer and Nohria (2000).
12. Raelin and Cataldo (2011).
13. Fink, Beak, and Taddeo (2011); Hannah, Uhl-Bien, Avolio, and Cavarretta (2009); Watkins (2009); Yukl (2013).
14. Grant and Mack (2004); Huy and Mintzberg (2003); Kets de Vries and Cheak (2014).
15. Krantz (2010).
16. Barsoux and Manzoni (1998); Kippenberger (1998).
17. Marks and De Meuse (2005).
18. Hwang and Lichtenthal (2000).
19. Hannah, Uhl-Bien, Avolio, and Cavarretta (2009); Hormann and Vivian (2005); Kahn, Barton, and Fellows (2013); Teo, Lee, and Lim (2017).
20. Benjamin and Mabey (1990); Hwang and Lichtenthal (2000).
21. Kahn, Barton, and Fellows (2013).
22. Guzman (2018); Kim and Mauborgne (2003b); Sugarman (2010).
23. Kim and Mauborgne (2003b).
24. Freedman (1996); Karsten, Keulen, Kroeze, and Peters (2009).
25. Freedman (1996).
26. Bruch and Ghoshal (2001); Bruch and Sattelberger (2001).
27. Bruch and Sattelberger (2001).
28. Ghosn (2002); Hughes, Barsoux, and Manzoni (2003); Millikin and Fu (2005); Tischler (2002); Thornton (1999).
29. Huy (2010).
30. Bruch and Sattelberger (2001).

31. Lorsch and McTague (2016).
32. Benjamin and Mabey (1990).
33. Huy (1999).
34. Huy and Shipilov (2012).
35. Benjamin and Mabey (1990); McKay (1997); Van der Voet, Groeneveld, and Kuipers (2014).
36. Bridges (2009).
37. Huy (2011); Huy (2018).
38. Kahn, Barton, and Fellows (2013).
39. Kahn, Barton, and Fellows (2013).
40. Kim and Mauborgne (1993); Kim and Mauborgne (2003a); Kippenberger (1998).
41. Brockner (2006); Kim and Mauborgne (2003a); Van der Heyden and Limberg (2007).
42. Kim and Mauborgne (1993); Kim and Mauborgne (2003a).
43. Beer, Eisenstat, and Spector (1990).
44. Hannah, Uhl-Bien, Avolio, and Cavarretta (2009).
45. Higgs and Rowland (2011); Van der Voet, Groenveld, and Kuipers (2014).
46. Keller and Aiken (2009).
47. Kets de Vries and Miller (1984).
48. Hammond, Keeney, and Raiffa (1998).
49. Stopford and Baden-Fuller (1990).
50. Hormann and Vivian (2005).
51. Dowds (n.d.); Hormann and Vivian (2005).
52. Kets de Vries (2010).
53. Huy, Corley, and Kraatz (2014); Kets de Vries (2010).
54. Grant and Mack (2004).
55. Kets de Vries and Korotov (2010); Obholzer (1996); Zaleznik (1997).
56. Higgs and Rowland (2011).
57. Eberly, Johnson, Hernandez, and Avolio (2013); Heifetz and Laurie (1997); Kets de Vries (2002); McKay (1997).
58. Beer and Nohria (2000); Higgs and Rowland (2011); Huy (2001).
59. Beer, Eisenstat, and Spector (1990); Higgs and Rowland (2011); Kets de Vries and Korotov (2010).
60. Hernandez, Eberly, Avolio, and Johnson (2011); Kilburg and Donohue (2011).
61. Higgs and Rowland (2011).
62. Hannah, Uhl-Bien, Avolio, and Cavarretta (2009); Van der Voet, Groeneveld, and Kuipers (2014).
63. Nembhard and Edmondson (2006); Waldman, Ramirez, House, and Puranam (2001).
64. Smit (2009).
65. Bökkerink and Couwenbergh (2018).

Chapter 3

1. Gabriel (2011).
2. Davis (1979).
3. Wildschut, Sedikides, Arndt, and Routledge (2006).
4. Gabriel (2011).
5. Ybema (2004).
6. Douglas (1987).
7. Gabriel (2011).
8. Gabriel (2011).
9. Douglas (1987).
10. Brown and Humphreys (2002).
11. Ybema (2010).
12. Creswell and Roth (2018).
13. Harris (1968).
14. Wolcott (2008).
15. Long and Harding (2013).
16. American Psychiatric Association (2013).
17. Creswell and Roth (2018).
18. Volkan (2009).
19. Lau and Murnighan (1998).
20. Van de Loo (2018).
21. Krantz (2010).
22. Schein (2002).
23. Edmondson (1999).
24. Gabriel (2011).
25. Douglas (1987).
26. Wildschut, Bruder, Robertson, van Tilburg, and Sedikides (2014).
27. Ybema (2004).
28. Gioia (1998).
29. Bridges (2009).
30. Heifetz, Grashow, and Linsky (2009).
31. Brannick and Coghlan (2007).

Chapter 4

1. Kets de Vries (2014c).
2. Kets de Vries (2014b).
3. Braun (2017).
4. Kets de Vries (2017).

5. Kets de Vries (2017).
6. Long (2013).
7. Kets de Vries (2014b).
8. Chamorro-Premuzic (2016).
9. McLagan (2013).
10. Kets de Vries (2014c).
11. Kets de Vries (2014c).
12. Kets de Vries (2014c).
13. Kets de Vries (2004).
14. Kets de Vries (2002).
15. McLagan (2013).
16. McLagan (2013).
17. McLagan (2013).
18. Braun (2017).
19. Krizan and Herlache (2018).
20. Braun (2017).
21. Braun (2017).
22. Kets de Vries (2014b).
23. Kets de Vries (2004).
24. Kets de Vries (2017).
25. Kets de Vries (2017).
26. Kets de Vries (2004).
27. Kets de Vries (2004).
28. Braun (2017).
29. Kets de Vries (2014c).
30. Braun (2017).
31. Nevicka, Hoogh, Vianen, and Velden (2013).
32. Braun (2017).
33. Jackson (2012).
34. Chamorro-Premuzic (2016).
35. Kets de Vries (2014c).
36. Kets de Vries (2014c).
37. Saqib and Arif (2017).
38. Kets de Vries (2014c).
39. Frankl (1984).

Chapter 5

1. Polkinghorne (1983).
2. Gephardt (2004).

3. Barkham and Barker (2010).
4. Long and Harding (2013).
5. Kets de Vries, Manfred, and Cheak (2014).
6. Major and O'Brien (2005).
7. Lyons, Pek, and Wessel (2017).
8. Major and O'Brien (2005).
9. Steele (1997); Steele and Aaronson (1995).
10. Major and O'Brien (2005).
11. Petriglieri (2011).
12. Petriglieri (2011); Lazarus and Folkman (1984).
13. Chang, Solomon, and Westerfield (2016); Lyons, Pek, and Wessel (2017).
14. Stryker and Serpe (1994).
15. Burke (1991).
16. Petriglieri (2011).
17. Petriglieri (2011).
18. Major and O'Brien (2005).
19. LeDoux (1996); Zajonic (2000).
20. Blascovich and Mendes (2000).
21. Petriglieri (2011).
22. Neimeyer, Prigerson, and Davis (2002).
23. Petriglieri (2011).
24. Lyons, Pek, and Wessel (2017).
25. Major and O'Brien (2005).
26. Petriglieri (2011).
27. Major and O'Brien (2005).
28. Petriglieri (2011).
29. Louis (1980).
30. Levy, Harmon-Jones, and Harmon-Jones (2018).
31. Chang, Solomon, and Westerfield (2016).
32. Chang, Solomon, and Westerfield (2016).
33. Andiappan and Dufour (2017).
34. Chang, Solomon, and Westerfield (2016).
35. Andiappan and Dufour (2017).
36. Chang, Solomon, and Westerfield (2016).
37. Levy, Harmon-Jones, and Harmon-Jones (2018).
38. Cunliffe and Coupland (2011).
39. Cunliffe and Coupland (2011).
40. Cunliffe and Coupland (2011).
41. Andiappan and Dufour (2017).
42. Cunliffe and Coupland (2011).
43. Petriglieri (2011).
44. Kets de Vries, Manfred, and Cheak (2014).

Chapter 6

1. Zehnder (2018).
2. Kets de Vries (2015).
3. Ascher and Tonies (2021).
4. Kleiner (2010).
5. Kegan and Lahey (2001).
6. Kets de Vries (2015).
7. Kets de Vries (2002).
8. Breuer and Freud (1895).
9. Driessen, Hegelman, Abbass, Barber, Dekker, Van, Jansman, and Cuijpers (2015).
10. Eppel (2018).
11. Johansson, Bjorklund, Hornborg, Karlsson, Hesser, Ljotsson, Rousseau, Frederick, and Andersson (2013).
12. Johansson, Bjorklund, Hornborg, Karlsson, Hesser, Ljotsson, Rousseau, Frederick, and Andersson (2013).
13. Eppel (2018).
14. Wegner and Smart (1997).
15. Damasio (2003).
16. Eakin (2003).
17. Eakin (2003).
18. Damasio and Carvalho (2013).
19. Khalsa, Adolphs, Cameron, Critchley, Davenport, and Feinstein (2018).
20. Khalsa, Adolphs, Cameron, Critchley, Davenport, and Feinstein (2018).
21. Levine (2010).
22. Van der Kolk (2014).
23. Substance Abuse and Mental Health Services Administration (2014).
24. Van der Kolk (2015).
25. Van der Kolk (2014).
26. Baumann (1986).
27. Tabibnia and Radecki (2018).
28. Pennebaker (1990).
29. Wegner (2011).
30. Park, Ayduk, and Kross (2015).
31. Pennebaker and Smyth (2016).
32. Segal, Chatman, Bogaards, and Becker (2001).
33. Lieberman, Eisenberger, Crockett, Tom, Pfeifer, and Way (2007).
34. Roemer and Orsillo (2008).
35. Cummings, Hayes, Saint, and Park (2014).
36. Pennebaker and Smyth (2016).
37. Pennebaker (2004).

38. Baum and Rude (2012).
39. Wegner (2011).
40. Pennebaker and Smyth (2016).
41. Pascual-Leone, Yeryomenko, Morrison, Arnold, and Kramer (2016).
42. Creswell (2013).
43. Creswell and Poth (2018).
44. Kets de Vries and Cheak (2014).
45. Kets de Vries (2014a).
46. Watson and Clark(1988).
47. Crawford and Henry (2004).
48. Pascual-Leone, Yeryomenko, Morrison, Arnold, and Kramer (2016).

References

American Psychiatric Association. 2013. *Diagnostic and Statistical Manual of Mental Disorders* (5th ed.). Arlington, VA: American Psychiatric Publishing.

Andiappan, M., and L. Dufour. 2017. "A Difficult Burden to Bear: The Managerial Process of Dissonance Resolution in the Face of Mandated Harm-Doing." *Journal of Business Ethics* 141, pp. 71–86.

Arnaud, G. 2012. "The Contribution of Psychoanalysis to Organization Studies and Management: An Overview." *Organization Studies* 33, no. 9, pp. 1121–1135.

Arnaud, G. 2012. "The Contribution of Psychoanalysis to Organization Studies and Management: An Overview." *Organization Studies* 33, no. 9, pp. 1121–1135, p. 1123.

Arnaud, G. 2012. "The Contribution of Psychoanalysis to Organization Studies and Management: An Overview." *Organization Studies* 33, no. 9, pp. 1121–1135, p. 1124.

Ascher, J., and F. Tonies. February 18, 2021. "How to Turn Everyday Stress Into 'Optimal Stress." *McKinsey Quarterly.*

Barkham, M., and M. Barker. 2010. In M. Barker, A. Vossler, and D. Langdridge. (eds). *Understanding Counselling and Psychotherapy.* London: Sage.

Barsoux, J.L., and J.F. Manzoni. 1998. "Procedural Justice in Action; Restructuring at Air France." *INSEAD Working Paper.* 98/04/AC/OB.

Baum, E.S., and S.S. Rude. February 14, 2012. "Acceptance-Enhanced Expressive Writing Acceptance-Enhanced Expressive Writing Prevents Symptoms in Participants With Low Initial Depression." *Science+Business Media.* LLC. Published online: 14 February 2012, Springer.

Baumann, G. 1986. "Writing Is a Technology That Restructures Thought in the Written Word: Literacy in Transition." *ed. Oxford Clarendon Press,* pp. 33–50.

Beer, M., and N. Nohria. 2000. "Cracking the Code of Change." *HBR's 10 Must Reads on Change* 78, no. 3, pp. 133–141.

Beer, M., R.A. Eisenstat, and B. Spector. 1990. "Why Change Programs Don't Produce Change." *Harvard Business Review* 68, no. 6, pp. 158–166.

Benjamin, G., and C. Mabey. 1990. "Organisational Transformation and the Self." *Management Education and Development* 21, no. 4, pp. 327–334.

Bion, W. 1989. *Experiences in Groups.* Hove: Routledge.

Blascovich, J., and W.B. Mendes. 2000. *Challenge and Threat Appraisals: The Role of Affective Cues.* In "Feeling and Thinking: The Role of Affect in Social Cognition. Studies in Emotion and Social Interaction." J.P. Forgas (ed.), pp. 59–82. New York, NY: Cambridge University Press. 2nd ser.

Bökkerink, I., and P. Couwenbergh. November 19, 2018. "Opstand Van Subtop ABN Amro Escaleert (Translation: Rebellion From Sub Top ABN Amro Escalates)." *Het Financieele Dagblad.*

Brannick, T., and D. Coghlan. 2007. "In Defense of Being "native": The Case for Insider Academic Research." *Organizational Research Methods* 10, no. 1, pp. 59–74.

Braun, S. 2017. "Leader Narcissism and Outcomes in Organizations: A Review at Multiple Levels of Analysis and Implications for Future Research." *Frontiers in Psychology* 8, no. 773, pp. 1–22. doi: 10.3389/fpsyg.2017.00773

Breuer, J., and S. Freud. 1895. "Studies on Hysteria." Retrieved from www.valas.fr/IMG/pdf/Freud-Oeuvre-traduction-anglaise.pdf (emphasis added).

Bridges, W. 2009. *Managing Transitions: Making the Most of Change* (3rd ed.). Philadelphia, PA: De Capo Press.

Brockner, J. 2006. "Why It's So Hard to Be Fair." *Harvard Business Review* 84, no. 3, pp. 122–129.

Brown, A.D., and M. Humphreys. 2002. "Nostalgia and the Narrativization of Identity: A Turkish Case Study." *British Journal of Management* 13, no. 2, pp. 141–159.

Bruch, H., and S. Ghoshal. 2001. "Lufthansa 2000: Maintaining the Change Momentum." *LBS business case.* Ref. LBS-CS01-001.

Bruch, H., and T. Sattelberger. 2001. "Lufthansa's Transformation Marathon: Process of Liberating and Focusing Change Energy." *Human Resource Management* 40, no. 3, pp. 249–259.

Burke, P.J. 1991. "Identity Processes and Social Stress." *American Sociological Review*, 56, pp. 836–849.

Carr, A., and Y. Gabriel. 2001. "The Psychodynamics of Organizational Change Management: An Overview." *Journal of Organizational Change Management* 14, no. 5, pp. 415–421.

Chamorro-Premuzic, T. November 29, 2016. "Why We Keep Hiring Narcissistic CEOs?" *Harvard Business Review Digital Articles*, pp. 2–4.

Chang, T.Y., D.H. Solomon, and M.M. Westerfield. 2016. "Looking for Someone to Blame: Delegation, Cognitive Dissonance, and the Disposition Effect." *The Journal of Finance.* LXXI, no. 1, pp. 267–302.

Chang, T.Y., D.H. Solomon, and M.M. Westerfield. 2016. "Looking for Someone to Blame: Delegation, Cognitive Dissonance, and the Disposition Effect." *Journal of Finance* LXXI, no. 1, p. 271.

Chang, T.Y., D.H. Solomon, and M.M. Westerfield. 2016. "Looking for Someone to Blame: Delegation, Cognitive Dissonance, and the Disposition Effect." *Journal of Finance* LXXI, no. 1, p. 272.

Coldwell, D., T. Joosub, and E. Papageorgiou. 2012. "Responsible Leadership in Organizational Crises: An Analysis of the Effects of Public Perceptions of Selected South African Business Organizations' Reputations." *Journal of Business Ethics* 109, no. 2, pp. 133–144.

Coutu, D.L. 2002. "The Anxiety of Learning, The HBR Interview." *Harvard Business Review* 80, no. 3, pp. 100–106.

Crawford, J.R., and J.D. Henry. September 01, 2004. "The Positive and Negative Affect Schedule (PANAS): Construct Validity, Measurement Properties and Normative Data in a Large Non-Clinical Sample." *British Journal of Clinical Psychology* 43, no. 3, pp. 245–265.

Creswell, J.W. 2013. *Qualitative Inquiry and Research Design: Choosing Among Five Approaches*, (4th ed.) p. 70.

Creswell, J.W., and C.N. Poth. 2018. *Qualitative Inquiry & Research Design: Choosing Among Five Approaches*, (4th ed.), p. 83.

Creswell, J.W., and C.N. Roth. 2018. *Qualitative Inquiry and Research Design: Choosing Among Five Approaches*. Thousand Oaks, CA: SAGE Publications.

Cummings, J.A., A.M. Hayes, D.S. Saint, and J. Park. January 01, 2014. "Expressive Writing in Psychotherapy: A Tool to Promote and Track Therapeutic Change." *Professional Psychology Research and Practice* 45, no. 5, pp. 378–386.

Cunliffe, A., and C. Coupland. 2011. "From Hero to Villain to Hero: Making Experience Sensible Through Embodied Narrative Sensemaking." *Human Relations* 65, no. 1, p. 65.

Cunliffe, A., and C. Coupland. 2011. "From Hero to Villain to Hero: Making Experience Sensible Through Embodied Narrative Sensemaking." *Human Relations* 65, no. 1, p. 68.

Cunliffe, A., and C. Coupland. 2011. "From Hero to Villain to Hero: Making Experience Sensible Through Embodied Narrative Sensemaking." *Human Relations* 65, no. 1, p. 83.

Cunliffe, A., and C. Coupland. 2011. "From Hero to Villain to Hero: Making Experience Sensible Through Embodied Narrative Sensemaking." *Human Relations* 65, no. 1, pp. 63–68.

Damasio, A., and G.B. Carvalho. February 2013. "The Nature of Feelings: Evolutionary and Neurobiological Origins." *Nature Reviews, Neuroscience* 14, p. 143.

Damasio, A.R. 2003. "Looking for Spinoza: Joy, Sorrow, and the Feeling Brain." *Orlando, Fla: Harcourt.*

Davis, F. 1979. *Yearning for Yesterday: A Sociology of Nostalgia.* New York, NY: Free Press.

Douglas, M. 1987. "How Institutions Think." London, England: Routledge and Kegan Paul.

Dowds, M. n.d. *Organizational Empowerment and Systems Psychodynamics.* Creationstep Inc. Publication.

Driessen, E., L.M. Hegelman, A.A. Abbass, J.P. Barber, J.J. Dekker, H.L. Van, E.P. Jansman, and P. Cuijpers. 2015. "The Efficacy of Short-Terms Psychodynamic Psychotherapy for Depression: A Meta-Analysis Update." *Clinical Psychology Review* 42, pp. 1–15.

Eakin, E. April 19, 2003. "I Feel, Therefore I Am." *The New York Times.* Retrieved from www.nytimes.com

Eberly, M.B., M.D. Johnson, M. Hernandez, and B.J. Avolio. 2013. "An Integrative Process Model of Leadership: Examining Loci, Mechanisms, and Event Cycles." *American Psychologist* 68, no. 6, p. 427.

Edmondson, A. June 1999. "Psychological Safety and Learning Behavior in Work Teams." *Administrative Science Quarterly*, pp. 350–383.

Eppel, A. 2018. *Short-Term Psychodynamic Psychotherapy*, p. 707. Retrieved from https://doi.org/10.1007/978-3-319-74995-2

Etchegoyen, R.H. 1991. *The Fundamentals of Psychoanalytic Technique.* London: Karnac Books.

Fink, S.L., J. Beak, and K. Taddeo. 1971. "Organizational Crisis and Change." *The Journal of Applied Behavioral Science* 7, no. 1, pp. 15–37.

Fotaki, M., and P. Hyde. 2014. "Organizational Blind Spots: Splitting, Blame and Idealization in the National Health Service." *Human Relations*, pp. 1–22.

Fotaki, M., and P. Hyde. 2014. "Organizational Blind Spots: Splitting, Blame and Idealization in the National Health Service." *Human Relations*, pp. 1–22, p. 4.

Fotaki, M., S. Long, and H. Schwartz. 2012. "What Can Psychoanalysis Offer Organization Studies Today? Taking Stock of Current Developments and Thinking About Future Directions." *Organization Studies* 33, no. 9, pp. 1105–1120.

Fotaki, M., S. Long, and H. Schwartz. 2012. "What Can Psychoanalysis Offer Organization Studies Today? Taking Stock of Current Developments and Thinking About Future Directions." *Organization Studies* 33, no. 9, pp. 1105–1120, p. 1106.

Frankl, V.E. 1984. *Man's Search for Meaning.* Washington Square Press.

Freedman, N. 1996. "Operation Centurion: Managing Transformation at Philips." *Long Range Planning* 29, no. 5, pp. 607–615.

Gabriel, Y. 2011. *Storytelling in Organizations.* Oxford, United Kingdom: Oxford University Press.

Gecas, V. 1982. "The Self-Concept." *Annual Review of Sociology* 8, pp. 1–33.

Gephardt, R. 2004. "What Is Qualitative Research, and Why Is It Important?" *Academy of Management Journal* 47, no. 4, pp. 454–462.

Ghosn, C. 2002. "Saving the Business Without Losing the Company." *Harvard Business Review* 80, no. 1, pp. 37–45.

Gioia, D.A. 1998. "From Individual to Organizational Identity." *Identity in Organizations: Building Theory Through Conversations* 11, pp. 17–31.

Grant, J.M., and D.A. Mack. 2004. "Preparing for the Battle." *Organizational Dynamics* 4, no. 33, pp. 409–425.

Guzman, Z. July 13, 2018. "Bill Bratton Reveals What His 'Biggest Mistake' Taught Him About Ambition." *CNBC*.

Hammond, J.S., R.L. Keeney, and H. Raiffa. 1998. "The Hidden Traps in Decision Making." *Harvard Business Review* 76, no. 5, pp. 47–58.

Hannah, S.T., M. Uhl-Bien,, B.J. Avolio, and F.L. Cavarretta. 2009. "A Framework for Examining Leadership in Extreme Contexts." *The Leadership Quarterly* 20, no. 6, pp. 897–919.

Harris, M. 1968. *The Rise of Anthropological Theory: A History of Theories of Culture*. New York, NY: T.Y. Crowell.

Heifetz, R.A., and D.L. Laurie. 1997. "The Work of Leadership." *Harvard Business Review* 75, pp. 124–134.

Heifetz, R.A., A. Grashow, and M. Linsky. 2009. *The Practice of Adaptive Leadership: Tools and Tactics for Changing Your Organization and the World*. Boston, MA: Harvard Business Review Press.

Hernandez, M., M.B. Eberly, B.J. Avolio, and M.D. Johnson. 2011. "The Loci and Mechanisms of Leadership: Exploring a More Comprehensive View of Leadership Theory." *The Leadership Quarterly* 22, no. 6, pp. 1165–1185.

Higgs, M., and D. Rowland. 2011. "What Does It Take to Implement Change Successfully? A Study of the Behaviors of Successful Change Leaders." *The Journal of Applied Behavioral Science* 47, no. 3, pp. 309–335.

Hormann, S., and P. Vivian. 2005. "Toward an Understanding of Traumatized Organizations and How to Intervene in Them." *Traumatology* 11, no. 3, pp. 159–169.

Hughes, K., J.L. Barsoux, and J.F. Manzoni. 2003. "Nissan's U-Turn." *INSEAD Business Case*. 08/2014-5059.

Huy, Q.N. 1999. "Emotional Capability, Emotional Intelligence, and Radical Change." *Academy of Management Review* 24, no. 2, pp. 325–345.

Huy, Q.N. 2001. "Time, Temporal Capability, and Planned Change." *Academy of Management Review* 26, no. 4, pp. 601–623.

Huy, Q.N. 2010. "Building Emotional Energy for Renewal: Nissan." *INSEAD Working Paper*.

Huy, Q.N. 2011. *Emotional Capital as Strategy*. INSEAD Handout.

Huy, Q.N. 2018. *Collective Emotions & Strategic Innovation*. INSEAD PowerPoint slides.

Huy, Q.N., and H. Mintzberg. 2003. "The Rhythm of Change." *MIT Sloan Management Review* 44, no. 4, pp. 79–85.

Huy, Q.N., K.G. Corley, and M.S. Kraatz. 2014. "From Support to Mutiny: Shifting Legitimacy Judgments and Emotional Reactions Impacting the Implementation of Radical Change." *Academy of Management Journal* 57, no. 6, pp. 1650–1680.

Huy, Q.N., and A. Shipilov. 2012. "The Key to Social Media Success Within Organizations." *MIT Sloan Management Review* 54, no. 1, pp. 73–81.

Hwang, P., and J.D. Lichtenthal. 2000. "Anatomy of Organizational Crises." *Journal of Contingencies and Crisis Management* 8, no. 3, pp. 129–140.

Jackson, E. 2012. "Why Narcissistic CEOs Kill Their Companies." Retrieved from www.forbes.com/sites/ericjackson/2012/01/11/why-narcissistic-ceos-kill-their-companies/#a32b3b6304b9

Johansson, R., M. Bjorklund, C. Hornborg, S. Karlsson, H. Hesser, B. Ljotsson, A. Rousseau, R.J. Frederick, and G. Andersson. 2013. "Affect-Focused Psychodynamic Psychotherapy for Depression and Anxiety Through the Internet: A Randomized Controlled Trial." Retrieved from www.researchgate.net/publication/249967959_Affect-focused_psychodynamic_psychotherapy_for_depression_and_anxiety_through_the_Internet_A_randomized_controlled_trial

Kahn, W.A., M.A. Barton, and S. Fellows. 2013. "Organizational Crises and the Disturbance of Relational Systems." *Academy of Management Review* 38, no. 3, pp. 377–396.

Karsten, L., S. Keulen, R. Kroeze, and R. Peters. 2009. "Leadership Style and Entrepreneurial Change: The Centurion Operation at Philips Electronics." *Journal of Organizational Change Management* 22, no. 1, pp. 73–91.

Kegan, R., and L. Lahey. November 2001. "The Real Reason People Won't Change." *Harvard Business Review*.

Keller, S., and C. Aiken. 2009. *The Inconvenient Truth About Change Management*. McKinsey & Company Publication.

Kets de Vries, M.F.R. (ed.). 1991. *Organizations on the Couch*. San Francisco, Jossey-Bass.

Kets de Vries, M.F.R. 2001a. *The Leadership Mystique: A User's Manual for the Human Enterprise*. New York, NY: Financial Times Prentice Hall.

Kets de Vries, M.F.R. 2001b. *Struggling With the Demon: Perspectives On Individual And Organizational Irrationality*. Madison: Psychosocial Press.

Kets de Vries, M.F.R. 2002. "Can CEOs Change? Yes, But Only If They Want to." *INSEAD Working Paper No. 2002/36/ENT*, pp. 1–60.

Kets de Vries, M.F.R. January 2004. "Putting Leaders on the Couch: A Conversation With Manfred F.R. Kets de Vries." *Harvard Business Review*, pp. 1–8. Retrieved from www.hbr.org

Kets de Vries, M.F.R. 2006. *The Leader on the Couch: A Clinical Approach to Changing People & Organizations*. San Francisco: Jossey-Bass.

Kets de Vries, M.F.R. 2009. *Reflections on Leadership and Character*. London: Wiley.

Kets de Vries, M.F.R. 2010. *Leadership Coaching and the Rescuer Syndrome: How to Manage Both Sides of the Couch*. INSEAD Working Paper.

Kets de Vries, M.F.R. 2014a. "Dream Journeys: A New Territory for Executive Coaching." *Consulting Psychology Journal: Practice and Research* 66, no 2, pp. 77–92.

Kets de Vries, M.F.R. 2014b. "Coaching the Toxic Leader." *Harvard Business Review*, pp. 1–11.

Kets de Vries, M.F.R. 2014c. "The Psycho-Path to Disaster: Coping With SOB Executives." *Organizational Dynamics* 43, pp. 17–26.

Kets de Vries, M.F.R. 2015. "Vision Without Action Is a Hallucination: Group Coaching and Strategy Implementation." *Organizational Dynamics* 44, pp. 1–8.

Kets de Vries, M.F.R. 2017. "How to Manage a Narcissist." *Harvard Business Review*, pp. 2–4.

Kets de Vries, M.F.R., and A. Cheak. 2014. "Psychodynamic Approach." In P.G. Northouse (ed.), *Leadership: Theory and Practice* (7th ed.), pp. 295–327. Sage.

Kets de Vries, M.F.R., and D. Miller. 1984. *The Neurotic Organization: Diagnosing and Changing Counterproductive Styles of Management.* San Francisco, CA: Jossey-Bass Incorporated Pub.

Kets de Vries, M.F.R., and D. Miller. 1985. "Narcissism and Leadership: An Object Relations Perspective." *Human Relations* 36, no. 6, pp. 583–601.

Kets de Vries, M.F.R., and K. Korotov. 2010. *Developing Leaders and Leadership Development.* INSEAD Working Paper.

Khalsa, S.S., R. Adolphs, O.G. Cameron, H.D. Critchley, P.W. Davenport, and J.S. Feinstein. June 2018. "Interoception and Mental Health: A Roadmap." *Biological Psychiatry: Cognitive Neuroscience and Neuroimaging* 3, no. 6, pp. 501–513.

Kilburg, R.R., and M.D. Donohue. 2011. "Toward a "Grand Unifying Theory" of Leadership: Implications for Consulting Psychology." *Consulting Psychology Journal: Practice and Research* 63, no. 1, pp. 6–25.

Kim, W.C., and R. Mauborgne. 1993. "Procedural Justice, Attitudes, and Subsidiary Top Management Compliance With Multinationals' Corporate Strategic Decisions." *Academy of Management Journal* 36, no.3, pp. 502–526.

Kim, W.C., and R. Mauborgne. 2003a. "Fair Process: Managing in the Knowledge Economy." *Harvard Business Review* 81, no. 1, pp. 127–136.

Kim, W.C., and R. Mauborgne. 2003b. "Tipping Point Leadership." *Harvard Business*

Kippenberger, T. 1998. "Building Trust and Co-Operation Through Fair Process." *The Antidote* 3, no. 4, pp. 33–36.

Kleiner, A. 2010. "The Thought Leader Interview: Manfred F.R. Kets de Vries." *Strategy + business, Thought Leaders* 59, Summer.

Kotter, J.P. 1995. "Leading Change: Why Transformation Efforts Fail." *Harvard Business Review* 73, no. 2, pp. 59–67.

Krantz, J. 2010. "Social Defences and Twenty-First Century Organizations." *British Journal of Psychotherapy* 26, no. 2, pp. 192–201.

Krizan, Z., and A.D. Herlache. 2018. "The Narcissism Spectrum Model: A Synthetic View of Narcissistic Personality." *Personality and Social Psychology Review* 22, no. 1, pp. 3–31.

Lau, D., and J. Murnighan. 1998. "Demographic Diversity and Faultlines: The Compositional Dynamics of Organizational Groups." *The Academy of Management Review* 23, no. 2, pp. 325–340.

Lazarus, R.S., and C. Folkman. 1984. *Stress Appraisal and Coping*. New York, NY: Springer-Verlag.

LeDoux, J.E. 1996. *The Emotional Brain: The Mysterious Underpinnings of Emotional Life*. New York, NY: Simon & Schuster.

Lehman, R., and E. van de Loo. 2016. *The Value Lurking in Your Leadership Unconscious*. https://knowledge.insead.edu/blog/insead-blog/the-value-lurking-in-your-leadership-unconscious-4974

Levine, P. 2010. *In an Unspoken Voice. How the Body Releases Trauma and Restores Goodness*, p. 49 (Kindle).

Levy, N., C. Harmon-Jones, and E. Harmon-Jones. 2018. "Dissonance and Discomfort: Does a Simple Cognitive Inconsistency Evoke a Negative Affective State?" *Motivation Science* 4, no. 2, pp. 95–108.

Lieberman, M.D., N.I. Eisenberger, M.J. Crockett, S.M. Tom, J.H. Pfeifer, and B.M. Way. January 01, 2007. "Putting Feelings Into Words: Affect Labeling Disrupts Amygdala Activity in Response to Affective Stimuli." *Psychological Science* 18, pp. 421–428. doi:10.1111/j.1467-9280.2007

Long, S. 2013. "Using and Creating Socioanalytic Methods." In S. Long (Ed.), *Socioanalytic Methods: Discovering the Hidden in Organisations and Social Systems*, pp. 307–314. London: Karnac.

Long, S., and M. Harney. 2013. "The Associative Unconscious." In S. Long (ed.), *Socioanalytic Methods: Discovering the Hidden in Organisations and Social Systems*, pp. 3–22. London: Karnac.

Long, S., and W. Harding. 2013. "Socioanalytic Interviewing." In S. Long (ed.), *Socioanalytic Methods: Discovering the Hidden in Organisations and Social Systems*, pp. 91–105. London: Karnac Books.

Lorsch, J.W., and E. McTague. 2016. "Culture Is Not the Culprit." *Harvard Business Review* 94, no. 4, pp. 96–105.

Louis, M. R. 1980. "Surprise and Sense Making: What Newcomers Experience in Entering Unfamiliar Organizational Settings." *Administrative Science Quarterly* 25, pp. 226–251.

Luborsky, L., and P. Crits-Cristoph. 1998. *Understanding Transference: The Core Conflictual Relationship Theme Method*. Washington, WA: American Psychological Organization.

Lyons, B.J., S. Pek, and J.L. Wessel. 2017. "Toward a "Sunlit Path": Stigma Identity Management as a Source of Localized Social Change Through Interaction." *Academy of Management Review* 42, no. 4, pp. 618–636.

Major, B., and L.T. O'Brien. 2005. "The Social Psychology of Stigma." *Annual Review of Psychology* 56, no. 1, p. 402.

Major, B., and L.T. O'Brien. 2005. "The Social Psychology of Stigma." *Annual Review of Psychology* 56, no. 1, pp. 393–421.

Marks, M.L., and K.P. De Meuse. 2005. "Resizing the Organization: Maximizing the Gain While Minimizing the Pain of Layoffs, Divestitures, and Closings." *Organizational Dynamics* 34, no. 1, pp. 19–35.

McDougal, J. 1985. *Theaters of the Mind: Illusion and Truth on the Psychoanalytic Stage*. New York, NY: Basic Books.

McKay, N.F. 1997. "Radical Corporate Change: What Seems to Work-What Doesn't?" *Business Forum* 22, no. 1, pp. 8–14.

McLagan, P.A. 2013. "Emerge From the Shadows." *T+D* 67, no. 9, pp. 36–40. Retrieved from http://ezproxy.insead.edu:80/login?url=https://search.ebscohost.com/login.aspx?direct=true&db=bth&AN=89970070&site=ehost-live

Millikin, J.P., and D. Fu. 2005. "The Global Leadership of Charlos Ghosn at Nissan." *Thunderbird International Business Review* 47, no. 1, pp. 121–137.

Neimeyer, R., H. Prigerson, and B. Davis. 2002. "Mourning and Meaning." *American Behavioral Scientist* 46, pp. 235–251.

Nembhard, I.M., and A.C. Edmondson. 2006. "Making It Safe: The Effects of Leader Inclusiveness and Professional Status on Psychological Safety and Improvement Efforts in Health Care Teams." *Journal of Organizational Behavior* 27, no. 7, pp. 941–966.

Neumann, J.E., and L. Hirschhorn. 1999. "The Challenge of Integrating Psychodynamic and Organizational Theory." *Human Relations* 52, no. 6.

Nevicka, B., A.H. Hoogh, A.E. Vianen, and F.S. Velden. 2013. "Uncertainty Enhances the Preference for Narcissistic Leaders." *European Journal of Social Psychology* 43, no. 5, pp. 370–380.

Obholzer, A. 1996. "Psychoanalytic Contributions to Authority and Leadership Issues." *Leadership & Organization Development Journal* 17, no. 6, pp. 53–56.

Park, J., O. Ayduk, and E. Kross. 2015. "Stepping Back to Move Forward: Expressive Writing Promotes Self-Distancing." *Emotion* 16. Washington, D.C. doi. 10.1037/emo0000121

Pascual-Leone, A., N. Yeryomenko, O.-P. Morrison, R. Arnold, and U. Kramer. September 01, 2016. "Does Feeling Bad, Lead to Feeling Good? Arousal Patterns During Expressive Writing." *Review of General Psychology* 20, no. 3, pp. 336–347.

Pearson, C.M., and J.A. Clair. 1998. "Reframing Crisis Management." *Academy of Management Review* 23, no. 1, pp. 59–76, p. 60.

Pearson, C.M., and J.A. Clair. 1998. "Reframing Crisis Management." *Academy of Management Review* 23, no. 1, pp. 59–76. p. 61.

Pennebaker, J.W. 1990. "Opening Up: The Healing Power of Confiding in Others." William Morrow & Co, 1st ed.

Pennebaker, J.W. 2004. "Writing to Heal: A Guided Journal for Recovering from Trauma & Emotional Upheaval." New Harbinger Publications, Inc; 1st edition.

Pennebaker, J.W., and J.M. Smyth. 2016. *Opening Up by Writing It Down. How Expressive Writing Improves Health and Eases Emotional Pain*, p. 77. [Kindle].

Petrieglieri, G. 2020. "F**k Science !? An Invitation to Humanize Organizational Theory." *Organization Theory* 1, pp. 1–18, p. 3.

Petrieglieri, G.P., and J.L. Petrieglieri. 2020. "The Return of the Oppressed: A Systems-Psychodynamic Approach to Organization Studies." *Academy of Management Annals 2020* 14, no. 1, pp. 411–449, p. 417.

Petrieglieri, G.P., and J.L. Petrieglieri. 2020. "The Return of the Oppressed: A Systems-Psychodynamic Approach to Organization Studies." *Academy of Management Annals 2020* 14, no. 1, pp. 411–449.

Petrieglieri, J.L. 2011. "Under Threat: Responses to the Consequences of Threats to Individuals' Identities." *Academy of Management Review* 36, no. 4, p. 644.

Petrieglieri, J.L. 2011. "Under Threat: Responses to the Consequences of Threats to Individuals' Identities." Academy of Management Review 36, no. 4, p. 647.

Petrieglieri, J.L. 2011. "Under Threat: Responses to the Consequences of Threats to Individuals' Identities." *Academy of Management Review* 36, no. 4, pp. 641–662.

Polkinghorne, D. 1983. *Methodology for the Human Sciences: Systems of Inquiry.* Albany: State University of New York Press.

Raelin, J.D., and C.G. Cataldo. 2011. "Whither Middle Management? Empowering Interface and the Failure of Organizational Change." *Journal of Change Management* 11, no. 4, pp. 481–507.

Roemer, L., and S.M. Orsillo. 2008. *Mindfulness- & Acceptance-Based Behavioral Therapies in Practice.* The Guilford Press.

Romanelli, E., and M.L. Tushman. 1994. "Organizational Transformation as Punctuated Equilibrium: An Empirical Test." *Academy of Management Journal* 37, no. 5, pp. 1141–1166.

Saqib, A., and M. Arif. 2017. "Employee Silence as a Mediator in the Relationship Between Toxic Leadership Behavior and Organizational Performance." *Journal of Managerial Sciences* XI, no. 03, pp. 83–104.

Schein, E. 2002. "The Anxiety of Learning." *Harvard Business Review* 80, no. 3, pp. 100–106.

Segal, D.L., C. Chatman, J.A. Bogaards, and L.A. Becker. 2001. "One-Year Follow-Up of an Emotional Expression Intervention for Bereaved Older Adults." *Journal of Mental Health and Aging.* 7, no. 4.

Smit, J. 2009. *The Perfect Prey, Ignorance and Arrogance at ABN AMRO*. Amsterdam: Prometheus.

Stacey, R.D., and C. Mowles. 2016. *Strategic Management and Organisational Dynamics*, 7th edition. Harlow, UK: Pearson.

Steele, C.M. 1997. "A Threat in the Air: How Stereotypes Shape Intellectual Identity and Performance." *Am. Psychol* 52, pp. 613–629.

Steele, C.M., and J. Aaronson. 1995. "Stereotype Threat and the Intellectual Test Performance of African Americans." *Journal of Personal and Social Psychology* 69, pp. 797–811.

Stopford, J.M., and C. Baden-Fuller. 1990. "Corporate Rejuvenation." *Journal of Management Studies* 27, no. 4, pp. 399–415.

Stryker, S., and R.T. Serpe. 1994. "Identity Salience and Psychological Centrality." *Social Psychology Quarterly* 57, pp. 16–35.

Substance Abuse and Mental Health Services Administration. 2014. "Trauma-Informed Care in Behavioral Health Services." *Treatment Improvement Protocol (TIP) Series 57. HHS Publication No. (SMA) 13-4801*. Rockville, MD: Substance Abuse and Mental Health Services Administration.

Suchman, A.L. 2011. "Organizations as Machines, Organizations as Conversations. Two Core Metaphors and Their Consequences." *Medical Care* 49, no. 12, pp. S43–S48.

Sugarman, B. 2010. "Organizational Learning and Reform at the New York Police Department." *Journal of Applied Behavioral Science* 46, no. 2, pp. 157–185.

Tabibnia, G., and D. Radecki. 2018. "Resilience Training That Can Change the Brain." *Consulting Psychology Journal: Practice and Research* 70, no. 1, pp. 59–88.

Teo, W.L., M. Lee, and W. Lim. 2017. "The Relational Activation of Resilience Model: How Leadership Activates Resilience in an Organizational Crisis." *Journal of Contingencies and Crisis Management* 25, no. 3, pp. 136–147.

Thornton, E. November 15, 1999. "Remaking Nissan: A long, Hard Day With Carlos Ghosn, The Foreigner Remaking Japan's Giant." *Business Week*.

Tischler, L. 2002. "The Road to Recovery." *Fast Company*, no. 60, p. 75.

Van de Loo, E. 2018. "Constellation Dynamics: Group Faultlines, Rackets and Managing Explosive Conversations [Powerpoint slides]."

Van der Heyden, L., and T. Limberg. 2007. "Why Fairness Matters." *International Commerce Review: ECR Journal* 7, no. 2, p. 93.

Van der Kolk, B.A. 2014. *The Body Keeps the Score. Brain, Mind, and Body in the Healing of Trauma*, p. 238. [Kindle].

Van der Kolk, B.A. 2015. *The Body Keeps the Score: Brain, Mind, and Body in the Healing of Trauma*. New York, NY: Penguin Books.

Van der Voet, J., S. Groeneveld, and B.S. Kuipers. 2014. "Talking the Talk or Walking the Walk? The Leadership of Planned and Emergent Change in a Public Organization." *Journal of Change Management* 14, no. 2, pp. 171–191.

Volkan, V.D. 2009. "Large-Group Identity: "Us and Them" Polarizations in the International Arena." *Psychoanalysis, Culture and Society* 14, pp. 4–15.

Waldman, D.A., G.G. Ramirez, R.J. House, and P. Puranam. 2001. "Does Leadership Matter? CEO Leadership Attributes and Profitability Under Conditions of Perceived Environmental Uncertainty." *Academy of Management Journal* 44, no. 1, pp. 134–143.

Watkins, M.D. 2009. "Picking the Right Transition Strategy." *Harvard Business Review,* 87, no. 1, pp. 46–53, p. 114.

Watson, D., L.A. Clark, and A. Tellegen. 1988. "Development and Validation of Brief Measures of Positive and Negative Affect: The PANAS Scales." *Journal of Personality and Social Psychology* 54, no. 6.

Wegner, D.M. January 01, 2011. "Setting Free the Bears: Escape From Thought Suppression." *The American Psychologist* 66, no. 8, pp. 671–680.

Wegner, D.M., and L. Smart. 1997. "Deep Cognitive Activation: A New Approach to the Unconscious." *Journal of Consulting and Clinical Psychology* 65. no. 6, pp. 984–995.

Wildschut, T., C. Sedikides, J. Arndt, and C. Routledge. 2006. Nostalgia: Content, Triggers, Functions. *Journal of Personality and Social Psychology* 91, no. 5, pp. 975–993.

Wildschut, T., M. Bruder, S. Robertson, W.A.P. van Tilburg, and C. Sedikides. 2014. "Collective Nostalgia: A Group-Level Emotion That Confers Unique Benefits on the Group." *Journal of Personality and Social Psychology* 107, no. 5, pp. 844–863.

Wolcott, H.F. 2008. *Ethnography: A Way of Seeing* (2nd ed.). Walnut Creek, CA: AltaMira Press.

Ybema, S. 2004. "Managerial Postalgia: Projecting a Golden Future." *Journal of Management Psychology* 19, no. 8, pp. 825–841.

Ybema, S. 2010. "Talk of Change: Temporal Contrasts and Collective Identities." *Organization Studies* 31, no. 4, pp. 481–503.

Yerushalmi, H. 1992. "Psychoanalytic Supervision and the Need to Be Alone." *Psychotherapy* 29, no. 2, pp. 262–268.

Yukl, G.A. 2013. *Leadership in Organizations* (8th ed.). New Jersey, NJ: Pearson Education.

Zajonic, R.B. 2000. "Feeling and Thinking: Closing the Debate Over the Independence of Affect." In J.P. Forgas (Ed.), *Feeling and Thinking: The Role of Affect in Social Cognition*, pp. 31–58. Cambridge University Press.

Zaleznik, A. 1997. "Real Work." *Harvard Business Review* 75, no. 6, pp. 53–59.

Zehnder, E. 2018. "The CEO: A Personal Reflection. Adapting to a complex world." Retrieved from https://ceostudy.egonzehnder.com/The-CEO-report-Egon-Zehnder.pdf

About the Authors

Ross Emerson

Founder, Ross Emerson Ltd.—Consulting, Coaching, & Advisory

Ross Emerson is a consultant and executive coach with over 30 years of business experience drawing from international roles in Canada, Japan, the United Kingdom, Monaco, and India. In addition to his own private coaching business serving clients around the globe, Ross provides senior executive coaching and consulting services through the LHH International Center for Executive Options in London, UK. He also coaches executives in the Kellogg-Schulich EMBA program, rated no. 2 in the world in 2020 by *The Economist*.

During a successful career in financial services spanning over 30 years, Ross held senior roles in financial services strategy, operational risk management, learning and development, global payments, wealth management, and enterprise leadership. In 2021, Ross was invited by the National Institute of Organisation Dynamics Australia to present his research at their annual Symposium themed "Not Knowing and Coming to Know: Methods of Inquiry in Unconscious (Hidden) Dynamics in Organisations." Also in 2021, Ross was nominated for an Ontario Premier's Award for success in business. In 2013 and 2014, Ross won Royal

Bank of Canada's Private Banking Gold Award given to the top enterprise leaders across Canada. Prior to that in 2009 and 2011, Ross won the Barclays Chairman's award for Individual Contribution to Monaco and to the Europe regions, respectively.

Ross holds an Honors BA degree in Politics from Western University, a Graduate Certificate in International Business from Seneca College, an MBA from the Schulich School of Business, and an Executive Master in Change degree (distinction) from INSEAD's program on organizational culture and change management. In October 2021, Ross commenced a PhD in Management Studies at King's College London.

James Hennessy

Senior Vice President, Federal Reserve Bank of New York
James Hennessy is a Senior Vice President in the Supervision Group at the Federal Reserve Bank of New York. Since 2014, he has led the New York Fed's Governance and Culture Reform Initiative.

James joined the Bank in 1992 as an attorney in the Legal Group, where he oversaw issues related to assets held by international monetary authorities at the New York Fed. He was the corporate secretary and chief of staff for two of its presidents during 1998 to 2006. Throughout the 2008 Financial Crisis, he managed the New York Fed's legal team advising on the rescue and restructuring of AIG. He joined the Supervision Group in 2011 and served as its Interim Head in 2021.

The aims of the New York Fed's Culture Initiative are to reduce incidences of misconduct in banking and to increase public trust in the financial services sector. Through leading the Initiative, James concluded that the diagnosis and attempted remediation of culture problems often ignores the underlying feelings driving human behaviors. To demonstrate the importance of such feelings, his chapter draws a portrait of the collective emotions of his own organization during a period of profound change.

James holds a BA degree in Philosophy from St. John's College, an MPhil in Anglo-Irish Literature from Trinity College, an MS from Columbia University School of Urban Planning, and a JD from Columbia University School of Law. He also holds an Executive Master in Change degree (distinction) from INSEAD's program on organizational culture and change management.

Fernanda Pomin

Managing Partner, Verità Desenvolvimento Organizacional
Fernanda Pomin is the owner of Verità Desenvolvimento Organizacional, which is a company focused on Leadership and Talent Development and Culture Transformation.

From 2006 to 2010, Fernanda was a Client Partner at Korn/Ferry International in São Paulo, accountable for the start-up and growth of the Leadership and Talent Consulting business unit in Brazil. Before joining the Korn/Ferry team, she worked for ABN AMRO Bank for nearly 10 years. During that period, she was responsible for Organizational Development, Talent Management, and Leadership Development. Her experience with the Bank also includes three years in the Regional Office for Latin America and two years as an expatriate in the Bank's head office in the Netherlands. Fernanda also worked for other multinationals such as Hay Group, ACCOR Group, and Price Waterhouse. During that phase, she specialized in Organizational Redesign, Competency Management, and Executive Development.

Having worked with change and leadership development since the very beginning of her career, Fernanda got more and more intrigued by the complexity of such processes. Looking for new and more effective ways to promote change, she decided to better understand the unconscious dynamics at play both in leaders and in organizations, as to be able to improve her knowledge and repertoire as a consultant.

Fernanda earned her MBA in Human Resources at Universidade de São Paulo and has a BA in Psychology by PUC São Paulo. She is a certified as a coach by the Integrated Coaching Institute, LeaderSource, and Lore International. She also holds an Executive Master in Change degree (distinction) from INSEAD's program on organizational culture and change management.

Ricardo Senerman

Cofounder, Chairman, and CEO of Sencorp S.A.
Founder and Chief Consultant of DEEP Consulting

Ricardo Senerman is the founder of DEEP Consulting, a company devoted to putting people and organizations in a track of accelerated growth by applying a mix of psychodynamic tools and interactions to discover what is unique and authentic in them.

In his professional life, he acts as Chairman and CEO of Sencorp, a real estate company based in Chile which he cofounded. Sencorp was awarded in 2020 first place as the best developer in Chile and LATAM, and top 20 in innovation and sustainability by *Euromoney* Magazine. Mr. Senerman is also presently Chairman of the Board at Valle Nevado, a ski resort considered among the best in Latin America (Forbes 2017), and recommended by *CNN* (2012) and the *New York Times* (2018).

Ricardo holds a BS in Civil Engineering at Universidad de Chile (maximum distinction) and an Executive Master in Change degree from INSEAD (distinction). His interests include C-suite coaching, board and executive teams' effectiveness, and personal leadership development. He is fluent in English and Spanish and is based in Santiago, Chile.

Elizabeth Florent Treacy

Senior Lecturer and Thesis Director, INSEAD Executive Degree Programs, Supervisor, Coach, and Consultant
Elizabeth Florent Treacy explores the fallow fields that lie between traditional business school theories and the system-psychodynamic approach to understanding life in organizations. Curious reverie leads her to integrate her academic research, teaching, and coaching perspectives in a

holistic approach. Emotional dilemmas and unconscious paradoxes in periods of organizational change are of particular interest. Her work focuses on:

Organizational change and the unconscious: the intemporal, simultaneous, and paradoxical dynamics that affect individuals and groups, during periods of disruption

Personality traits and technostress: individuals' perceptions of stressors related to digital and virtual workspaces

Psychodynamic approach to academic writing projects: the interface between self-efficacy and psychological safety, and the ability to conceive and complete academic projects

Written narratives in leadership development: the role of emergent written narratives in leadership identity work

In her role as Senior Lecturer and Thesis Director, she works with executives to develop solid bridges between academic studies and real-world application. She is an accomplished author and book series editor, having authored or coauthored seven books, multiple academic articles in peer-reviewed journals, and prize-winning MBA case studies. She has presented her work in many academic and practitioner conferences, including the Academy of Management and the International Leadership Association. She put her own name on her organizational consultancy, in order to signal her sense of personal responsibility to her clients.

Originally from California and a long-time resident of France, Elizabeth feels privileged to have the best of both worlds. She holds a BA in Sociology from the University of California, Davis; an MS in Organizational Development from Fielding Graduate University; and an MA (Distinction) in INSEAD's Executive Master in Coaching and Consulting for Change; and she is currently finalizing her PhD dissertation. She has also earned a Certificate in Coaching and Consulting Supervision from the Tavistock Institute of Human Relations, London.

Theo van Iperen

Managing Partner, Giotto Management Consultants

Theo van Iperen is married to the love of his life, Floor, and father to their two beloved daughters, Zara and Eefje. He lives in the flower bulb region of the Netherlands, where every year in spring the fields turn into patchworks of colorful tulips, as far as the eyes can reach.

Theo is a management consultant for over 25 years and mainly concerned with empowering the workforce of organizations in bringing their competencies to full growth. From a humble background, he intuitively always felt it wasn't right for organizations to have bosses governing over their workforces. As a consultant, he experienced that organizations where leaders dared to embrace uncertainty and engage their workforce in realizing dramatic change were much more successful than classical top-down led organizations.

But as a trained economist—raised in its vocabulary of activity-based costing, benchmarking, and targets—it took him quite some time to understand the hidden dynamics making the difference within organization. His curiosity to understand these brought him to the Executive Master in Change program at INSEAD, where the concept of systems psychodynamics, concentrating on the undercurrents within people and organizations, turned out to be pivotal for him. Concepts like emotional capital, relational systems theory, and fair process gave words and logic to his intuition and personal experiences as a consultant. This journey ended up in his contribution to this book about the restoration of troubled organizations and a new book in Dutch from his hand about the same topic, released in 2021.

And the learning in this field still continues for Theo, now as a PhD candidate trying to contribute by combining his personal experiences as a consultant with new scientific research.

Index

OTHER TITLES IN THE SERVICE SYSTEMS AND INNOVATIONS IN BUSINESS AND SOCIETY COLLECTION

Jim Spohrer, IBM, and Haluk Demirkan, University of Washington, Tacoma, Editors

- *Service in the AI Era* by Jim Spohrer
- *Emerging FinTech* by Paul Taylor
- *The Emergent Approach to Strategy* by Peter Compo
- *Compassion-Driven Innovation* by Nicole Reineke, Debra Slapak, and Hanna Yehuda
- *Adoption and Adaption in Digital Business* by Keith Sherringham and Bhuvan Unhelkar
- *Customer Value Starvation Can Kill* by Walter Vieira
- *Build Better Brains* by Martina Muttke
- *ATOM, Second Edition* by Kartik Gada
- *Designing Service Processes to Unlock Value, Third Edition* by Joy M. Field
- *Disruptive Innovation and Digital Transformation* by Marguerite L. Johnson
- *Service Excellence in Organizations, Volume II* by Fiona Urquhart
- *Service Excellence in Organizations, Volume I* by Fiona Urquhart
- *Obtaining Value from Big Data for Service Systems, Volume II* by Stephen H. Kaisler, Armour, and J. Alberto Espinosa
- *Obtaining Value from Big Data for Service Systems, Volume I* by Stephen H. Kaisler, Armour, and J. Alberto Espinosa

Concise and Applied Business Books

The Collection listed above is one of 30 business subject collections that Business Expert Press has grown to make BEP a premiere publisher of print and digital books. Our concise and applied books are for...

- Professionals and Practitioners
- Faculty who adopt our books for courses
- Librarians who know that BEP's Digital Libraries are a unique way to offer students ebooks to download, not restricted with any digital rights management
- Executive Training Course Leaders
- Business Seminar Organizers

Business Expert Press books are for anyone who needs to dig deeper on business ideas, goals, and solutions to everyday problems. Whether one print book, one ebook, or buying a digital library of 110 ebooks, we remain the affordable and smart way to be business smart. For more information, please visit www.businessexpertpress.com, or contact sales@businessexpertpress.com.

CPSIA information can be obtained
at www.ICGtesting.com
Printed in the USA
JSHW030022151022
31618JS00004B/70